RAW VEGAN EASY HEALTHY RECIPES

SIMPLE, LOW-FAT, HEALTH INFUSING CUISINE

BY JOHN McCABE

Author of

Igniting Your Life:
Pathways to the Zenith of Health and Success

Sunfood Traveler:
Global Guide to Raw Food Culture

Sunfood Diet Infusion:
Transforming Health through Raw Veganism

Vegan Myth Vegan Truth:
*Obliterating Rumors and Lies about
the Earth-Saving Diet that can Save Your Life*

Carmania Books

Raw Vegan Easy Healthy Recipes
Simple, Low-Fat, Health-Infusing Cuisine

Disclaimer:

This book is sold for information purposes only. How you interpret and utilize the information in this book is your decision. Neither the author nor the publisher and/or distributor will be held accountable for the use or misuse of the information contained in this book. This book is not intended as medical advice because the author and publisher of this work are not recommending the use of chemical drugs or surgery to alleviate health challenges. It also does not stand as legal advice, or suggest that you break any laws. Because of the way people interpret what they read, and take actions based on their own intellect and life situations, which are not in the author's, publisher's, and/or distributor's control, there is always some risk involved; therefore, the author, publisher, and/or distributor of this book are not responsible for any adverse effects or consequences from the use of any suggestions, foods, substances, products, procedures, or lifestyles described hereafter.

ISBN: 978-1-884702-10-5

First Edition: 2013

Cover photo: Rich Marchewka, Marchewka.com

Published by:

Carmania Books

POB 1272, Santa Monica, CA 90406-1272, USA

TABLE OF CONTENTS

1   Introduction
5   Go Organic
11   Localizing Your Food
19   Sprouting
25   Cultured and Fermented Foods
29   Enzymes
35   Fiber
39   Leaky Gut (Damaged Intestinal Lining)
        Syndrome, Celia, Crohn's, Irritable Bowel
        Syndrome, Intestinal Issues, Reflux, Heartburn,
        Gluten Intolerance, Candida, Skin Conditions,
        and Arthritis
47   Steps Toward Better Digestion and Nutrition:
        Soaking and Activating Nuts, Seeds, Beans,
        and Grains
55   Dehydrated Foods
59   Sea Vegetables
65   Wild Foods
69   The Soy Fiasco
73   Read Labels
75   Eggs, Fish Oil, and Human Disease
83   Plant-based Foods and Health
93   Humans are Herbivores,
        not Carnivores or Omnivores
97   Plant-based Diet is the Way to Health
103   A Plea for Natural Foods Systems
109   If You are not Growing a Food Garden...
113   Kitchens

115	Kitchen Equipment
121	Kitchen Food Stock
127	Recipe Books

131 Random Recipes for a Raw Vegan Kitchen
SALADS

132	Simple Salad
132	Kale Salad Basics
134	Simple Kale Salad
135	Kale Salad for Four
136	Fancy Kale Salad
137	Einstein Salad
139	Voona Salad
140	Sliver Salad
141	Carrot Fennel Salad
142	Cucumber Salad
143	Corn Salad
144	Fettuccini Alfredo

DRESSINGS, SAUCES, SALSA, SPREADS, MARINARA, GRAVY

145	Tahini Dressing
145	Herbal Sunflower Cream Dressing
146	Ranch Dressing
147	Creamy Avocado Dressing
149	Caesar Dressing
149	Apple-Grape Vinaigrette
150	Creamy Salad Dressing
151	Cool Cilumber Dressing
151	Citrus-Ginger Dressing
152	Almond Ginger Dressing
152	Simple Dressing
153	Alfredo Salad Dressing
154	Chunky Corn Salsa
155	Fresh Tomato Salsa
155	Naise Spread
156	Sundried Tomato Butter

157 Matboukha
158 Pine Nut Spread
159 Marinara
160 Gravy

HUMMUS

161 Rocking Raw Hummus
163 No Bean Hummus
163 Xam's Hummus

WRAPS

165 Ingredient Ideas for Wraps
168 Mushroom Wrap Filler

SIDES

169 American Wild Rice Pilaf
170 Pressed Red Cabbage Caraway Slaw
171 Sea Vegetable Slaw
171 Marinated Mushrooms
172 CauliRice
173 Mashed Not Potatoes
174 Hemp Seed Tabouli
174 Megan Elizabeth's Falafels
176 Raw Curry Falafel

BURGERS, LOAFS, STUFFED PEPPERS

177 Sunfood Burgers
179 Veggie Nut Loaf (or burgers)
180 Veggie Loaf with Gravy
181 Stuffed Red Bell Peppers

FIESTA

183 Taco Filler
184 Dehydrating onions, celery, and bell pepper
185 Taco Salad Ingredient Ideas
185 Spiced dehydrated pumpkin seeds
186 Pico de Gallo
186 Sour Cream
187 Raw Unfried NoBeans
188 Raw Corn Chips or Shells

190   Raw Chia Fresca for Four
191   Raw Vegan Flan

PATÉ

193   Cabbage Pumpkin Seed Paté
193   Vegetable Paté
194   Mexican Paté
195   Indian Paté

CHIPS AND CRACKERS

197   Zucchini Chips
197   Hemp Corn Chips
198   Dehydrated Crackers

SOUPS

201   Tomato Soup
201   Carrot Soup
202   Catch A Healthy Habit Spinach Soup
203   Pumpkin Soup
204   Chilled Tomato Soup with Avocado Salsa
206   Cream of Broccoli Soup

DESSERTS

207   Carrot Cake
208   Carrot Cake Icing
209   Apple Cobbler
210   Pie Crust
210   Fruit Pie Crust
211   Fruit Pie Filling
212   Fig Berry Dessert
213   Strawberry-Banana Dessert
214   Peach or Strawberry Teacup Tarts
215   Fruit Pudding
215   Chia Seed Pudding
216   Lemon Pudding
216   Frozen Vanilla Yogurt
218   Raw Ice Cream
218   Cantaloupe Mint Sorbet
219   Simple Carob Truffles
220   Traveling Truffles

222   Carob Sauce
222   Carob Crumble

BREAKFAST

224   Monomealing
225   Simple Breakfast
225   48 Hour Breakfast

DRINKS, MYLKS, SMOOTHIES, AND JUICES

227   Simple Nut Milk
228   Holiday Nog
229   Brazil Hemp Milk
229   Banana Nut Smoothie
230   Basic Green Smoothie
231   Spirulina Smoothie
231   Blue Green Smoothie
232   Liver Cleanse Smoothie
232   Strawberry-Peach Smoothie
233   Peachie Smoothie
233   Zing Smoothie
234   Mango Orange Spinach Smoothie
234   Warming Savoury Green Smoothie
235   Turquoise Barn Green Smoothie
235   Winter Green Smoothie
236   Melon-Mint Cocktail
236   Veggie Juice Basics
239   Green Drink
240   Green Power Morning Juice
240   Runner's Drink

i   About the Author

       What People are saying about *Igniting Your Life*

       Living Light Culinary Institute
       Samudra

INTRODUCTION

While so many recipe books are filled with pretty photos, it isn't the photos that get me to buy the books. It's the recipes. If the recipes aren't what I want, I don't care what else is in the book.

About ten years ago, I bought one of those fancy, expensive, hardcover recipe books filled with very nice photography of the raw vegan cuisine the recipes seemed to appear to represent.

While trying to make the recipes for a dinner party, I realized that most of the measurements were off. Not just a little. A lot. So much so that if anyone followed the recipes, the dishes would clearly not turn out the way they appeared in the photos. Nowhere near how they appeared in the photos.

The recipes in that book were also complicated, some taking several days to prepare. They included dehydrated things and soaked things and fermented things and sprouted things and things that needed to be left overnight, and so forth. When it was time to combine things, it became very obvious that there was far too little of some things and far too much of others. Unlike how I usually work in the kitchen, with these recipes, I measured everything just as the book suggested. And, it was a disaster.

I ended up meeting one of the co-authors of the book. When I asked her if she knew that the measurements in the recipes were mostly off, she flippantly told me, "Well, that was meant to be a coffee table book anyway, not something you would really use in your kitchen."

Really?

So, they put out an expensive recipe book that wasn't really supposed to be a recipe book. If they wanted to put out

1

a book of pretty photos of foods, why not simply do that, and leave out the recipes that were more like guesswork and not tested for accuracy?

For this book, I am simply leaving out any fanciness. There are no photos or illustrations misrepresenting what the recipes would appear as. Instead, I'm presenting a variety of recipes that I have made.

I mostly rely on organic ingredients, but if I really want something that I can't get organic, I'll settle for non-organic.

I grow some of my own foods in an organic garden. I compost all of my organic food scraps into soil by way of compost pits, burying the scraps a few times per week.

In addition to my garden, I get ingredients from farmers' markets, an independent natural foods store, and a fruit wholesaler. I have friends who grow food, and we share some of what we grow.

We often eat very simply, such as salads, smoothies, juices, and simple meals. Our kitchen doesn't have pre-packaged meals, or canned or bottled things. There are no microwavable frozen things. There is no microwave, grill, fryer, or even a dishwasher. The oven of the old stove is used for storage.

Sometimes, I monomeal, which is eating one thing for a meal – such as a bunch of tangerines. I think that is a good way to calm down the digestive system and provide unadulterated, raw, organic nutrients. I find that the days I monomeal end up being days in which I experience a lift in energy.

Sometimes I do the gourmet raw thing, which can involve recipes that can be complicated to make, with a variety of ingredients. I find that I don't feel as vibrant if I eat that way very often.

I don't eat at restaurants much, as I often find the food to be oily and salty. Uncooked food can have what I guess can best be described as a high-vibe. If you are eating some dish that has a variety of ingredients, and all of them are buzzing with their raw energy, the digestive tract could end up feeling a bit overwhelmed.

Mostly, I eat low fat. Except for an occasional bit of raw organic hempseed oil or raw organic coconut oil, I'm not into using bottled oils. There hasn't been a bottle of olive oil here in several years. Other oils, like canola and corn, are never considered.

We don't use much salt, which is something that started happening several years ago. Once you stay away from salt, when you do eat something with it the salt flavor can end up overwhelming other flavors in the dish.

This raw vegan diet thing is something I sort of naturally picked up. As I was a teenager I started spending days eating only fruit and berries that I picked from a former farm that had gone wild, and also from vegetables and vine fruits that I grew in my garden. I realized that when I ate only those things I felt incredible and had plentiful amounts of energy.

In the winters I would go back into eating mostly cooked food and some animal products, and I would get the common "seasonal" illnesses. I would look forward to summer so that I could feel amazing again.

Eventually, as an adult I ended up writing vegan books and helping other authors write their vegan books.

Sometime in the 90s I started using the term "raw vegan." I didn't know that the term was going to be used so widely. I didn't know that I was going to become known for that simple little decision, as the guy who "coined the term." Today you can do an Internet search for "raw vegan," and you can remain on the computer for weeks reading up about the diet, who is following it, the benefits of it, ways of doing it less successfully, ways of doing it more successfully, and so forth. There are blogs and videos and social media sites, all dedicated to raw veganism.

I also didn't know that the books I was working on, including my books and the books that I had helped others to write, were going to be so widely read.

I continually get mail and email from people living all over the planet. As the reader feedback increased, I found that I was being too generous with the amount of time I was spending to respond to reader mail. At one point I had to stop spending so much time responding. It was taking up way too much time and I wasn't getting the things done that I needed to get done, and I wasn't spending enough time with the important people in my life.

If you write me a letter, know that I probably got it, but I really don't have time to stop and reply every time I get one – there are things I need to be doing, projects I need to be working on, and people with whom I need to spend time.

For additional information about the raw vegan diet, see my other book, *Sunfood Diet Infusion*. In it, I provide a whole lot of information beneficial to learning about the benefits and purposes of the raw vegan diet.

If you want to take your raw vegan culinary expertise to the professional level, I encourage you to get to the Living Light Culinary Arts Institute in Northern California. It is there where you can spend several weeks gaining the skills needed to become a professional raw vegan chef, which is a trade that is increasingly popular.

With so many raw vegan and raw vegan fusion (raw and cooked vegan food) restaurants opening around the world, a person with the right skills can literally work themselves around the world, including in restaurants, retreat centers, catering companies, at certain resorts, on some cruise ships, and even in the homes of certain wealthy people. Living Light Culinary Institute provides the training and certification a person needs if they are to truly be a raw vegan chef. (Access: **RawFoodChef.com**)

Meanwhile, I hope you find this book to be a good little addition to your kitchen. I will likely overhaul the manuscript in future years so that it is reflective of whatever else I have learned that could be helpful to the book.

Before we get to the recipes, I want to share some information about food and how it gets to your table.

GO ORGANIC

IF you do not know what Monsanto is doing to the food plants of the planet through genetic engineering, chemically-grown foods, and putting farmers under contract, you need to learn.

If you think that what Monsanto is doing, what Bayer CropScience and other genetic engineering companies are doing, and what toxic farming chemicals are doing do not impact you, think again. These companies are impacting everything from the trees in the mountains to the fish at the bottom of the seas... to your body cells.

What Monsanto and other GMO companies are doing with their combination of genetically altered plants and toxic faming chemicals not only impacts the food, it also alters the soil organisms, the water, the air, and your hormonal balances (in all animals, not just the human animal). The genetically altered organisms and farming chemicals end up in the land and water.

The chemicals being used on common monocropped foods cause cancer, birth defects, miscarriages, learning disabilities, and nerve disorders. They alter hormonal balances, and trigger or contribute to obesity and diabetes. They alter the way your brain performs, the way your heart beats, and the way your cells function.

The Winter 2012 edition of Earth Island Journal (**EarthIslandJournal.org**) contains a couple of interesting articles about Monsanto and Bayer CropScience. Here are some quotations from there:

"The World Health Organization estimates that every year at least 3 million people – and as many as 25 million people –

are poisoned by pesticides, and at least 40,000 people are accidentally killed by them."

"A recent study by the US Geological Office has found significant levels of Roundup in the air and waterways in two US farm states – Iowa and Mississippi. According to USGS researcher Paul Capel, glyphosate (the active ingredient in Roundup) was detected in every stream sample taken in Mississippi over a two-year period and in most of the air samples taken. 'It is out there in significant levels; it is out there consistently.' Capel says. 'So people are exposed to it through the air.'" ...

"Use of the herbicide has skyrocketed in recent decades due mostly to the popularity of Roundup Ready GM crops. The USGS says that more than 88,000 tons of glyphosate were applied in the US in 2007, up from 11,000 tons in 1992." ...

"Persistent exposure could alter endocrine pathways, leading to obesity, heart problems, and diabetes."

For more information about genetically modified food plants and toxic farming chemicals, access the Web site to the Organic Consumers Association: **OrganicConsumers.org**.

Here is a list of sites and organizations providing information about organic gardening, organic farming, and the dangers of genetically modified foods, farming chemicals, and the impact these toxic chemicals and genetically altered food plants are having on Nature.

Beyond Pesticides, **BeyondPesticides.org**
Bioneers, **Bioneers.org**
Co-op Directory, **CoOpDirectory.org**
Food Consumer, **FoodConsumer.org**
Farm to Consumer Legal Defense Fund,
   FarmToConsumer.org
Gardenerd, **Gardenerd.com**
Local Harvest, **LocalHarvest.org/store/local-csa.jsp**
Monsanto Watch, **MonsantoWatch.org**

Non-GMO Shopping Guide, **NonGMOShoppingGuide.com**
Organic Consumers Association, **OrganicConsumers.org**
Organic Foodee, **OrganicFoodee.com**
Organic Its Worth It, **OrganicItsWorthIt.org**
Organic Seed Alliance, **SeedAlliance.org**
Pesticide Action Network, **PANNA.org**
Real Food Challenge, **RealFoodChallenge.org**
Rodale Institute, **RodaleInstitute.org**
The War on Bugs, **TheWarOnBugsBook.com**
Worldwide Opportunities on Organic Farms, **WWOOF.org**

Learn about organic gardening and organic farming.

Support local independent organic food stores (NOT that Wall Street darling, Whole Foods Market).

Support community supported agriculture (CSA) groups.

Find local organic food co-ops. Or start a co-op, like Kristina Carrillo-Bucaram did in Texas with the Rawfully Organic Food Co-op.

One of the best things you can do to be healthier is to plant and maintain a food garden.

So many people spend money trying to have the perfect lawn, spending more money and water and energy on that than they would if they would grow a veggie garden and have some fruit trees. They'd save water, money, and time, including the time it takes to make the money to pay for the water, pay for the veggies and fruit they purchase, and the time it takes to shop. It is so much easier to go outside and harvest some fresh food at the peak of its ripeness and rich in nutrients, rather than to have to go to a store to purchase fading food that is days or weeks old.

In their modern living of the encapsulating cities and suburbs, most people are completely reliant on stores and restaurants for food, a system that can quickly collapse. It's a system of food delivery that has given rise to terrible companies like Monsanto and BayerCrop Science, that are developing suicide seeds, patenting food plants, suing farmers and placing farmers under contract to only plant patented suicide seeds; and creating some of the most toxic chemicals on Earth to use on farms, and that end up in our bodies, and in the bodies of domesticated and wild animals.

A neighbor told me, "Gardening is filthy." Yes, proud woman, and where does your food come from? Leave it up to those filthy farmers. You are so much better than them!

"The glory of gardening: hands in the dirt, head in the sun, heart with nature. To nurture a garden is to feed not just the body, but the soul."
– Alfred Austin

The simple act of gardening improves your health in ways uncommonly known. Skin exposed to the beneficial mycobacterium vaccae in soil triggers the brain to release serotonin, improving mood, assisting the uptake of nutrients in the gut, and boosting the immune system (Neuroscience journal, April 2007). Also, the harvesting and smell of fresh fruits and vegetables triggers the release of dopamine in the brain. Dopamine is a feel-good chemical associated with feelings of bliss and euphoria.

If you want to change the world, change what you put into your mouth, and your choices of where you get that food.

CommunityGarden.org
EdibleForestGardens.com
FallenFruit.org
FoodIsPower.org
FoodNotLawns.com
GardeNerd.com
IslandSeed.com
KitchenGardners.org
NeighborhoodFruit.com
RareSeeds.com
SavingOurSeed.org
SeedAlliance.org
SeedSavers.org
SquareFootGardening.com

VictorySeeds.com
VeggieTrader.com
Yards to Gardens, **Y2G.org**

Monsanto is the company that made Agent Orange, Aspartame, Bovine Growth Hormone, DDT, Glyphosate, PCBs, and Saccharine. Those products have been linked to devastating health problems, including cancers, birth defects, nerve disorders, and miscarriages.

When you support organic farmers and maintain an organic home garden, you are NOT supporting Monsanto and other chemical companies that are wreaking havoc on the health of humans, wildlife, and the environment, poisoning our land, water, and air, and destabilizing family farm culture around the globe.

Please, support organic farmers.

LOCALIZING YOUR FOOD

"There are many reasons to buy locally grown food. You'll get exceptional taste and freshness, strengthen your local economy, support endangered family farms, safeguard your family's health, and protect the environment.

Getting to know the farmers who grow your food builds relationships based on understanding and trust.

Fruits and vegetables shipped from distant states and countries can spend as many as seven to fourteen days in transit before they arrive in the supermarket."

– **FoodRoutes.Org**

"Supporting local, ecologically sound agriculture is one step we can take toward achieving a more sustainable lifestyle. Buying locally grown food conserves fuel and reduces pollution by shortening shipping distances. Local food is also fresher, and therefore tastier and more nutritious. Choosing organically grown food provides for the conservation of our valuable agricultural soils. Supporting local farmers contributes toward preservation of the rural character of the New England landscape."

– **FarmDirectCoOp.Org**

THE primary way you can help to restore and protect not only nature, but also the world as a whole, is through your food choices.

The way we live in modern society depends on airplanes, boats, trains, trucks, and other forms of transportation to ship foods. The less you rely on foods from distant lands, the better it is for the environment.

11

Why are you eating apples grown five thousand miles from where you live? Why are you eating spinach grown three thousand miles away? Why are you drinking orange juice from oranges grown in Italy when you live in Australia? Why are you eating grapefruit grown in Australia when you live in Arizona? Why are you eating almonds grown in California when you live in Italy, where almonds also grow? Why are you eating grapes from California when you live in China? Why are you eating cherries from Canada when you live in Japan? Why are you eating lettuce grown in California when you live in Florida? Why are you drinking wine from South Africa when you live in France, or California wine when you live in Argentina? Why is most of the food you eat arriving in containers consisting of paper made from trees chopped down in forests, and plastic made from crude oil drilled from Earth? Why are you filling a trash bag with food packaging every two days? Why are you eating food that was grown using toxic chemical fertilizers, pesticides, defoliants, fungicides, biocides, herbicides, miticides, and insecticides, and that contains food dyes, preservatives, flavorings, and other synthetic chemicals made from petroleum, coal, and other substances obviously not natural to the human diet? Why do the foods you eat contain synthetic vitamins with cyanide residue, or substances that increase the risk of lung cancer, nerve disorders, hormonal imbalances, mood swings, and birth defects? Why are you eating genetically engineered plant substances? Why are you eating fruits and vegetables that have been coated with wax and/or shellac? Why are you purchasing foods that you can grow yourself?

An interesting book on how corporate food is produced and transported is *Tangled Routes: Women, Work, and Globalization on the Tomato Trail*, by Deborah Barndt. The book details the route of a corporate-grown tomato from a Mexican farm to a consumer in Canada.

Consider what it takes in resources to grow, ship, package, market, and prepare the food you eat. Then think of ways along the entire path your food takes in which you can make your diet more Earth-friendly.

Begin seeking foods that are grown within your foodshed. Your foodshed is the region of the world where you live – generally a circle of about one to six hundred miles surrounding you. Closer is better.

With many types of food shipped thousands of miles before they are eaten, it makes environmental sense to choose to make the largest part of your diet consist of foods that are grown within a few hundred miles of where you live. Some people describe this way of eating locally grown foods as being a "locavore."

Choosing to purchase and consume locally grown foods will reduce fossil fuel use. It also will contribute to your community. This is because you will be supporting local farms.

Large food companies have been taking over the food industry as people rely more on commercial foods and become less involved with growing their own. If you also grow some of your food, which is encouraged, you can further reduce dependence on fossil fuels as well as on multinational corporations that are destroying the planet.

Another benefit of localizing your fruit and vegetable choices, especially by growing some of your own food, is that you will eat them when they are at or closer to their peak of ripeness, when they are rich in nutrients.

Eating fruits and vegetables when they are truly ripe will also prevent the consumption of natural plant chemicals produced as defense mechanisms. These chemicals are called salicylates and protect plants from insects, birds, and other wildlife. Salicylates also work to protect the plants from bacteria and fungi. They become naturally less present in ripe fruits and vegetables.

Salicylates can build up in people who continually eat unripe fruits and vegetables, and can trigger emotional issues, such as depression, fatigue, hyperactivity, and lack of attention and concentration. While it is unlikely that you will avoid all salicylates and there are some naturally present in some of the foods you eat, those with histories of headaches and asthma may also want to steer clear of foods and products rich in salicylates. Other physical reactions indicating salicylate sensitivity can include itchy and puffy eyes, nausea, stomach upset, rashes, sinus issues, and swelling in the feet and/or hands. Salicylism, which is an overexposure to salicylates, is similar to aspirin poisoning. Aspirin is a salicylate-based drug, and can cause a pharmacological reaction in people sensitive to salicylates. Because salicylates may also be used in preservatives, perfumes, and some medications, those with sensitivity to salicylates would benefit by steering clear of those products.

While you may be consuming some salicylates when you eat fruits and vegetables, there is an amount that the system can easily tolerate, but continually consuming unripe fruits and vegetables can be problematic. Some people are more sensitive to salicylates than others. Eating whole fruits and vegetables, even unripe ones, is not going to expose a person to the amounts of salicylates contained in processed and packaged foods made from unripe fruits and vegetables, such as jams and jellies made using unripe fruit, orange juice made using unripe oranges, or tomato sauces or catsup made using unripe tomatoes. The salicylates would be much more present in the pureed and or boiled down concentrated foods, because there would be many more tomatoes in a cup of tomato sauce when compared to a cup of chopped fresh tomatoes.

Fruits and vegetables that have been shipped from far away, and may have been picked while they were not yet ripe, often have ripening agents applied to them, such as bethylene, ethylene gas, ethane, ethephon, and calcium carbide, when arriving in the destination country to trigger the ripening process. Because the residues of ripening agents may not be the healthiest things to consume, it could be beneficial to use vinegar and water to rinse, soak, or otherwise wash fruits and vegetables that have arrived from distant countries.

Calcium carbide releases acetylene gas, which triggers the ripening of fruit. Acetylene has been found to reduce oxygen transfer to the brain, but is found in such small amounts when used as a ripening agent that it has been determined a nonissue. The reason calcium carbide has been banned as a ripening agent in some countries is because it can contain trace amounts of arsenic and phosphorus, which can end up as residues on produce.

One reason why truly fresh, locally grown and ripe fruits and vegetables may taste better than those that have been shipped in from far away is because of the artificial ripening processes that the shipped fruits and vegetables may have gone through.

Fruits and vegetables that may be treated with ripening agents include apples, beets, bell peppers, blackberries, blueberries, cherries, citrus fruits, cranberries, currants, figs, mangoes, papayas, pears, and tomatoes. Coffee is also often treated with ripening agents.

This is not to say that you should avoid all fruits and vegetables that are from outside of your region, especially if those are the only fruits available to you. It is important to have fruits and vegetables in your diet. But, it is more beneficial to eat the actual fruits and vegetables, rather than processed foods containing fruits and vegetables, such as canned and bottled products – or jellies or jams. If you can't get fruits and vegetables that are whole and unheated, another choice would be to use dehydrated fruits and vegetables. The last choice would be to use the canned and jarred products.

Another way to improve the quality of your food is to avoid produce that has been genetically engineered.

Look for the term "non-GMO" on food labels. GMO is the abbreviation for *genetically modified organism*. Companies that label their foods as non-GMO are aiming to supply food that has not been genetically modified. A good source for information on this is the National Family Farm Coalition, a group working with many other farm organizations to stop the spread of GE (genetically engineered) agriculture (Access: NFFC.Net/Issues/GEIssues.html).

The activities of the companies that are genetically engineering food plants are a danger to everyone. Some of the companies include Aventis (France), BASF (Germany), Bayer CropScience (Germany), DOW Chemical (US), DuPont (US), Monsanto (US), Novartis (Swiss), and Zeneca (Britain). The very same companies are also involved in the manufacture of dangerous farming chemicals that poison our food, water, soil, and air, and alter microorganisms, including the good bacteria in our stomachs. Why are we allowing this to happen? The way you spend your food money is either supporting these companies, or not. (Access: **MonsantoWatch.org, OccupyMonsanto360.org, OrganicItsWorthIt.org, SayNoToGMOs.org, LabelGMOs.org, ResponsibleTechnology.org**, and **OrganicConsumers.org**)

Refrain from eating foods that were grown using toxic chemical fertilizers, insecticides, herbicides, pesticides, fungicides, miticides, defoliants, and other farming chemicals. Refuse genetically engineered foods. Seek organically grown foods and you will be reducing the use of toxic chemicals while supporting the growing organic foods industry.

While you may not be able to localize all of your food choices, you can certainly do so with most of the foods you eat. The more you eat organically grown and locally grown food, and the less you eat foods that were transported from distant lands, the more you will be improving the level of your nutrition while protecting wildlife and the ecosystems of both your region and the rest of the planet. It also protects farm workers from toxic farming chemicals.

Becoming a "food artisan" by growing your own organic food garden is one of the best things you can do for the environment. You will reduce packaging, because there won't be any on the food you grow. You will improve your level of nutrition, because freshly grown food is more nutritious than food that has been shipped and stored. You will save money. You will get exercise and sun exposure. You can give away the food that is more than you can eat. And you will be opting out of the globalized, industrialized, supermarketized, corporatized, and increasingly genetically engineered food industry.

"Food is an intimate act. Food is not only our most intimate and powerful and profound connection with

nature, with a larger order, it is also our most powerful
and intimate connection with our culture."
  – Dr. Will Tuttle, author of *The World Peace Diet*,
  WorldPeaceDiet.org

The simple act of gardening improves your health in ways
uncommonly known. Skin exposure to the beneficial
Mycobacterium vaccae in soil triggers the brain to release
serotonin, improving mood, assisting the uptake of nutrients
in the gut, and boosting the immune system (*Neuroscience*
journal, April 2007). Also, the harvesting and smell of fresh
fruits and vegetables triggers the release of dopamine in the
brain. Dopamine is a feel-good chemical associated with
feelings of bliss and euphoria. Again, more reasons to
maintain an organic food garden.

"The glory of gardening: hands in the dirt, head in the
sun, heart with nature. To nurture a garden is to feed not
just the body, but the soul."
  – Alfred Austin

See my book *Sunfood Traveler: Global Guide to Raw Food
Culture* for more information about gardening, seed saving,
heirloom seeds, farming, and sustainable food culture groups
working to create a more sustainable culture, such as Food
Not Lawns, Lawns to Gardens, and Eat the View. An
interesting book on the topic of localizing your food is Brian
Halweil's *Eat Here: Homegrown Pleasures in a Global Supermarket*.
There is also the book *Food Not Lawns*.

Learn about wild edible plants, including dandelion,
Lambsquarters, minor's lettuce, purslane, mustard greens, and
other wild greens that are rich in nutrients. Go to YouTube
and search for the video series: Wild Edibles with Sergei
Boutenko. Sergei also is the author of a book on wild foods to
be published in 2013.

"The single largest contributor to global depletion is
the raising, slaughtering, and eating of animals – over 700
billion livestock animals and 1-2 trillion fish (some

researchers have estimated as many as 1.7 trillion chickens are raised and slaughtered in one year)."

– **ComfortablyUnaware.com**

"Anyone who isn't vegan simply doesn't comprehend what we've done to nonhumans – sentient beings just like us. They don't get the language, the sentiment, the horror. And it is a horror. For we have taken everything from them: their homes, their children, their land, their families, their dignity, their joy, their sanity, their liberty, and their lives. Try telling that to your average meat eater, and watch them glaze over."

– Sienna Blake

SPROUTING

"Scientists have studied sprouts for centuries to better understand their high levels of disease-preventing phytochemicals, and how they contribute to better health, from prevention to treatment of life-threatening diseases. Major organizations including the National Institutes of Health, American Cancer Society and Johns Hopkins University have reinforced the benefits of sprouts with ongoing studies that explore various sprout varieties for their nutritional properties and to validate health claims.

According to Paul Talalay, M.D., in the American Cancer Society *NEWS*, 'broccoli sprouts are better for you than full-grown broccoli, and contain more of the enzyme sulforaphane which helps protect cells and prevents their genes from turning into cancer.' His findings are consistent with several epidemiologic studies that have shown that sprouts contain significant amounts of vitamins A, C and D. Sprouts are widely recognized by nutrition-conscious consumers and health care professionals as a 'wonder food.'"

– *Good Sprout News* of the International Sprout Growers' Association; ISGA-Sprouts.Org

E ATING fresh sprouts is an excellent way to get phytonutrients (plant nutrients), such as enzymes (vital to all life), amino acids (for building protein), chlorophyll (abundant in greens, especially baby greens), biophotons (vital nutrients that are tiny specks of light in living cells that play a role in cell communication, and referred to by raw foodists as *vital life-force energy* or *galama*), and other trace nutrients.

Sprouting both increases the nutrients in the seeds and makes other nutrients in the seeds more available.

Sprouting is one of the least expensive ways, besides growing your own garden, to get raw greens into your diet, which is important for anyone wanting to experience vibrant health.

People often use the term *sprouts* to define both *germinated* seeds and true sprouts. You may hear people say *sprouted garbanzo hummus*, which is really germinated garbanzo hummus. Germinated seeds are those that have been soaked to enliven enzymes, or grown only until a small tail of a root appears. A sprout is a seed brought past the germination stage and an early leaf is starting to form, or leaves are present, such as alfalfa sprouts, sunflower sprouts, mung bean sprouts, and sprouted wheatgrass.

But people seem to have a thing against the word *germinate*, and maybe because it reminds them too much of the word *germ*, so they will continue to use the word *sprout* for both sprouted and germinated seeds. Some of the seeds that are germinated rather than sprouted include buckwheat, garbanzo, chia, and quinoa. Some seeds are used both as germinates and as sprouts, such as sunflower, mung bean, and lentil.

There are also *soaks,* which are seeds or nuts that have been soaked a number of hours to turn off the enzyme inhibitors and ignite the enzymic activity – spurring the formation of a variety of nutrients. There are also many raw recipes calling for *soaked* seeds or nuts, such as *soaked* macadamia nuts, *soaked* pignolis (pine nuts) or *soaked* sunflower seeds. People that follow a *living foods diet* are sure to soak all the nuts and seeds before they eat them, rather than eating unsoaked raw seeds and nuts, which *live foodists* consider not fully alive. Soaking makes nuts and seeds more nutrient-rich and easier to digest. Raw almonds, macadamias, cashews, Brazil nuts, and hazelnuts are commonly used by raw foodists after the nuts have been soaked.

The magic of a seed is that it is a plant-making kit. Seeds are amazing in that they can be eaten by an animal, pass through the digestive tract, and start to grow only after they have left the animal's digestive tract. Magically, what seeds need to grow is provided in the animal's nutrient-rich poop. That is how many plants are spread through nature, by being eaten by animals, who then unknowingly provide themselves as a vehicle to transfer the seed to a new location, where it grows.

Exposing seeds to moisture takes the seed out of its dormant state, shutting off the enzyme inhibitors, which mostly exist in the skin or shell, and igniting the nutrient factories that build the structure from a seed into a plant. The first few days of a plant's life is a time of exuberant energy and a microscopic storm of nutrient-making activity. By consuming soaks, germinates, and sprouts, you are transferring the concentrated vibrant nutrients of the young plant into your body.

As long as you have an area that is between about 50 to 100 degrees Fahrenheit, and that has indirect sunlight, you can grow sprouts anywhere on the planet (although some seeds are more likely to grow better when in the temperature range of between 60 and 90 degrees Fahrenheit). You don't need anything special to grow sprouts. All it takes is something like a big glass jar and a screen to cover the top. You can also use a bowl covered with a screen, a sheer cloth, towel, or a plate. Of course, you also need clean water to first soak the seeds, then to rinse them. We often germinate seeds in a bowl covered by a plate, which also makes it easy to rinse as we put water in the bowl, then hold the plate on with my thumbs as we tip the bowl over the sink or outside, and let the water seep out.

A common method of growing sprouts is to use a big jar covered by a screen, and keeping the jar tilting almost upside down at an approximate 45° angle in a big bowl to drain excess water.

Some people use mesh bags to sprout seeds. This also makes it easy to rinse the seeds. Certain seeds, especially small seeds, such as millet and flax, germinate better this way, and are easier to rinse.

21

When I talk of soaking seeds, I'm not speaking of chia seeds. Chia seeds are so small that the only real way to germinate them is in a bowl, or a jar with a fine screen – only rinsing them once – if you rinse them at all (I don't). They germinate within minutes – forming an enzyme-rich gel. They are good to use for mixing with fresh-cut fruit salad and they will germinate from the moisture of the fruit. They can also be put into smoothies or juices. Stirring or blending chia into nut or seed mylks provides a nice, silky, creamy texture. People who make kombucha sometimes put chia in the kombucha just minutes or hours before drinking it. Chia kombucha is also something that a lot of natural foods stores are selling.

There are a variety of sprouting trays and machines on the market that can make it easier to sprout seeds. Some sprouters automatically spray and rinse the sprouts. I've never owned one of those gizmos. Some people like them. We do fine with bowls and jars. Sprouting isn't rocket science.

There are a variety of seeds that are good for sprouting. Seek those that are from organic sources – such as at your local natural foods store.

Make sure your soaking and sprouting bowls, jars, screens, and/or mesh bags are clean, or else you may also find that you will be growing some unwanted bacteria – turning your sprouts rancid.

During the soaking time, remember that seeds can die if they remain in water too long. The soak times vary according to the temperature of the room and water. If it is cold, you may want to soak seeds for a longer period, such as a day; if it is warm you want to soak them for a shorter period – such as a few hours. In warmer weather the seeds will also need to be rinsed more often. Sprouting also takes place faster in a brighter location. As you get more familiar with sprouting, you will learn what works best for the types of seeds you are using, and the environment of the room.

Unless you have an automatic sprouting machine that regularly mists the seeds, you will need to rinse them one to three times per day with water to keep them clean, fresh, and hydrated (moist). It is good to have fine mesh sprouting bags, or a screened strainer for rinsing the smaller seeds, and a colander with small holes for rinsing the larger seeds/beans.

Sprouts benefit from exposure to light, such as indirect sunlight, as this will trigger the development (photosynthesis) of nutritious chlorophyll in the sprouts.

Within a plant, chlorophyll transforms sunlight and CO_2 into sugar and oxygen. Chlorophyll is molecularly very similar to human blood plasma. There are strong nutritional qualities in chlorophyll as it helps strengthen the immune system in fighting off infections, and helps rid the body of toxins, especially those that gather in the liver. Because chlorophyll helps generate new cell growth, it also assists in healing wounds and illnesses.

Some sprouts are more chlorophyll-rich than others. With a content of about 70 percent chlorophyll, wheatgrass is perhaps the richest sprout of all.

If you are not going to use the sprouts right away, you can slow their growth by putting them in the refrigerator, or in a cold room (not freezing). Rinse and drain once a day with clean water and you should be able to keep them in a cold, slowed growing state for two to four days, and sometimes longer.

You can also slow soaked seeds from sprouting fully by keeping them in the refrigerator. Then, when you are ready to sprout them, remove them from the refrigerator, rinse, and let them grow at room temperature.

Sprouts are living, breathing plants. They need air. Don't put them into a sealed container. A screened jar or a casserole dish with a glass top works well because they both allow for air to enter the container. A jar with a screen fastened around the top and turned upside down at an angle works best for many seeds because it prevents them from sitting in water while also letting in air. As they sprout at room temperature, remember to rinse them two or three times a day, and drain excess water to keep them from rotting.

One way of keeping sprouts fresh in the refrigerator is to store them in a bamboo bowl covered by a second bamboo bowl that has a dozen or more small holes drilled into it. This also provides an easy way to rinse them once a day by pouring water into the bowl, covering with the top bowl, and tilting upside down over the sink or outside to eliminate excess water before putting them back into the refrigerator.

Some people use a piece of clean, moist hemp fabric or hemp cloth bag to wrap sprouts (and green leaf vegetables), placing them on a plate or a bowl, and keeping them in the refrigerator this way for up to a couple of days. Hemp fabric should be used, and not cotton (likely to contain pesticides), and not synthetic fabrics.

Some people will drink the soak water as it contains enzymes (made of amino acids, the building blocks of protein) that are released by the seeds. Lemon or apple juice added to the enzyme-rich soak water makes it taste better.

Just as long as the soaked seeds are kept moist and you don't let them dry out, you break down the enzyme inhibitors, and nurture the seed to become a plant.

When the sprouts have reached the size you want them, put them in indirect sun for an hour covered with a thin cloth. By doing this you will ignite the chlorophyll and nutrient-making factory within the sprouts, greatly increasing their nutritional value. Make sure not to allow sun to bake them or let them dry out. Keep them covered with the sheer cloth to keep little buggy friends away.

> "Vegetarian food leaves a deep impression on our nature. If the whole world adopts vegetarianism it can change the destiny of humankind."
> – Albert Einstein

CULTURED AND FERMENTED FOODS

CULTURED foods can be highly nutritious, rich in enzymes, and provide healthful probiotic bacteria (L. acidophilus, L. bifidus, etc.) that gather in our intestines as intestinal flora. These bacteria help us to assimilate nutrients provided by other foods, bring the system into healthy pH balance, and work as part of the immune system.

Fermentation helps to break down complex proteins into the simpler amino acid compounds, making them easier to digest for those with a digestive tract that has been weakened by sickness or years of bad diet.

To experience vibrant health you need to have a population of good bacteria taking up residence in your intestines. A good base of intestinal flora is important for our immune system; helps fight off bad bacteria that cause disease; provides and creates nutrients, such as the B-complex vitamins; and provides for healthy elimination of toxins. Fermented vegan foods provide these.

Cultured foods include the traditional Korean food called kimchi (also *kimchee*) made from vegetables; and also sauerkraut, which is from Eastern Europe and is made from cabbage. Kombucha tea is a cultured food. Miso, a salty paste traditionally made from soybeans, is a cultured food. (Make sure it is made from raw beans, or make it yourself. It can also be made from almonds, chickpeas, or brown rice.) Raw apple cider that has been fermented is also a cultured food, as is wine.

Some raw foodists don't consume vinegar, soy products, or wine. Some raw foodists also do not consume fermented

25

foods of any type as they consider fermented foods to be less than vibrant, and they may also avoid salted foods. I sometimes eat fermented foods, such as kombucha, truly raw sauerkraut, and foods that might contain apple vinegar. I usually don't use salt, but will sometimes eat at raw restaurants where many of the foods do contain salt. I usually avoid anything containing soy. But, I'm not as pure as some other people attempt to be.

Cultured foods are relatively easy to make and they rely on cultures that are naturally present in the air. They can also be made using a nondairy source of kefir culture, or vegan probiotic powder.

When you make cultured foods, do so under sanitary conditions to avoid mold and harmful bacteria that can spoil your creation. Also, use organically grown raw vegetables, not those that have been heated, boiled, or otherwise cooked.

When making fermented foods, the area where the crock or other container sits should be out of direct sunlight, in an area free from dust and disturbance, and where the container can remain for several days as the food ferments (some people ferment kimchi and sauerkraut for up to several weeks, and even longer – but start simple, and learn from there). By doing an Internet search, or at your local library, you can find information about how to make fermented foods.

Some raw food restaurants are making fermented foods, including kimchi, kombucha, and sauerkraut. Some raw food restaurants give classes in fermenting.

Be aware that many types of cultured foods sold in stores have been pasteurized (heated) before they are jarred, for longer shelf life. Heating destroys many of the nutrients.

If you purchase cultured food, make sure the labels clarify the foods as "unpasteurized" or "raw vegan." These will be found in the refrigerated section.

Cultured foods, in their unheated state, are becoming more popular in natural foods stores. Kombucha is one example of this It may contain alcohol. If you purchase Kombucha, seek out brands that don't contain pasteurized fruit juice.

You can also make cultured seed and/or nut cheeses by mixing soaked pine nuts, almonds, macadamia, or others blended with nutritional yeast, and cultured rejuvelac water or powdered vegan probiotic powder. This raw vegan cheese can be used soft, or dehydrated over 24 hours to make a flaky cheese similar to Parmesan. If you use salt, don't add any until after the cheese has been aged for a day, or just before you dehydrate it, if you are making the flaky or dried cheese. The soft cheese can also be flavored with dried tomatoes, or with herbs, such as dill, rosemary, oregano, or basil. (See Renée Loux's book, *Living Cuisine*.)

A tool helpful in making fermented foods is a kimchi crock. They are often sold in Asian markets. It has a moat-like lip around the edge that gets filled with water so that the lid fits into this lip, preventing air from getting in, but allowing fermenting gas to escape.

Never eat food that you are unsure about. If the fermented food you are making ends up smelling rotten rather than tangy, and especially if the vegetables turn brown or even black, toss them away.

ENZYMES

"What is the great secret that has been eluding the investigations of scientists and lives of laypersons for centuries? Enzymes. You are only alive because thousands of enzymes make it possible. Every breath you take, thought you think, or sentence you read, is a result of thousands of complex enzyme systems and their functions operating simultaneously."

– Ann Wigmore, author of *The Hippocrates Diet*

"Enzymes are substances that make life possible. They are needed for every chemical reaction that takes place in the human body. No mineral, vitamin, or hormone can do any work without enzymes. Our bodies, all our organs, tissues, and cells are run by metabolic enzymes."

– Dr. Edward Howell, *Enzyme Nutrition*

"Through years of research Dr. Ann Wigmore discovered that all the enzymes, vitamins, and minerals that the body needs are found within the foods we eat – if these foods are prepared in such a way as to maintain or unlock their life-giving nutrients."

– Creative Health Institute,
CreativeHealthUSA.Com/LivingFoods.htm.

THE standard American diet ("SAD" diet) is lacking in useful enzymes. This is because heating and intense processing of food damages enzymes, which are key to a diet fueling vibrant health.

You may hear some raw food proponents say that enzymes contain the *life-force energy* of the plant. Well, the plant would not have life if you took away any of a number of components in the plant, such as the minerals, the water, the biophotons, or one of the varieties of amino acids in the plant. Enzymes are protein, and proteins are composed of amino acids. Because so many components, including electrical charges, biophotons, antioxidants, omega-3 fatty acids, certain vitamins, and other nutrients, are present in raw plant matter compared to food that has been cooked at high temperatures, and these components work in combination with each other, it is easy to understand that undamaged enzymes and the proteins they are made of are only part of the combination of substances that improve health when a person follows a plant-based diet consisting of mostly or all raw foods.

> "The act of cooking – and the resultant loss of nutrients, enzymes, and oxygen – impairs our digesting and elimination, which are the two most controlling factors of nutrient absorption that regulate our metabolism."
> – Dr. Brian Clement, HippocratesInst.org

The more your diet consists of a variety of enzyme-rich raw plant matter, the more likely you are of experiencing vibrant health.

When I hear someone say that unheated fruits and vegetables contain "life-force energy," I don't simply consider the enzymes. I think of the whole variety of nutrients, electrical charges, and biophotons.

Biophotons are little specs of light that disappear when a plant is cooked. In his 1956 book, *The Sunfood Way to Health*, Dugald Semple wrote, "Cooking devitalizes food, as when we kill seeds by boiling them, and thus causes the sun energy or galama in the plant cells to be dissipated." Semple was using the words of George Julius Drews who wrote about galama in his 1912 book *Unfired Foods and Tropho-Therapy*. I believe the modern-day term both Drews and Semple would have used for that sun energy *galama* they spoke of is *biophotons*. They also understood what many people still today don't seem to understand, that raw foods contain a nutrient that cooked foods do not: biophotons, which people can call *galama*.

It is interesting that the tissues of the body, including the brain, contain photoreceptor proteins that interact with light. We are meant to eat unheated plant matter, which contains the microscopic specs of light. Enzymes also contain both biophotons and electrical charges.

Enzymes are necessary for life. All living things form and contain enzymes. There are thousands of types of enzymes in the body. They are made up of protein molecules and are paramount to all chemical reactions within the body. They act along with minerals, fats, carbohydrates, vitamins, and all other necessary components of the body tissues to produce living functions throughout the body. Enzymes are central to the formation, repair, restoration, and revitalization of all tissues.

If you do not have a healthy bank of enzymes within your body, and don't continue to get them from raw fruits and vegetables, your health degrades.

People who consistently consume raw plant matter have a better store of enzymes in their bodies than those who eat a diet that is made up of cooked food.

There are three classes of enzymes: metabolic enzymes, digestive enzymes, and food enzymes.

The first class, metabolic enzymes, are within the cells of the body tissues. They are essential to all cellular activity, including breathing, healing, and movement.

The second-class, digestive enzymes, are produced by all areas of the alimentary tract, from the mouth through the stomach and intestines to the colon. Amylase enzymes are essential to the digestion of carbohydrates. Lipase enzymes are essential to the digestion of fats. Protease enzymes are essential to the digestion of proteins.

The third class, which are essential to the formation of both metabolic and digestive enzymes, are food enzymes. These are supplied to the body through raw plant substances.

Enzymes exist in all plant life. They are essential to the ripening of food. There are some plants that survive in areas where temperatures get above 120 degrees, such as some types of cacti and palm trees, but in large measure, most plants die (because their enzymes are greatly damaged) at temperatures above 120 degrees. Freezing food may damage enzymes. Also, there are some plants that exist in areas where temperatures drop well below freezing, but again, most plants on the planet die when temperatures drop below freezing – while others do not.

Because fermenting of raw foods, such as in raw sauerkraut, kimchi, and seed cheeses, increases enzymatic activity, some people encourage the use of fermented foods for healing of the body. The late Dr. Ann Wigmore, a raw food enthusiast and author of several books, advocated the use of fermented foods in healing the body.

Also, as noted elsewhere in the book, soaking raw nuts and seeds activates the enzymes while greatly increasing both the digestibility of the nuts and seeds and the nutrient content of them.

When a person's diet is lacking in raw plant matter, the digestive enzymes degrade and begin to draw on the metabolic enzymes. This series of events weakens the body, causes sluggishness, and helps pave the way for illness to set in. The standard American diet of low quality foods creates a human who is no place near peak health. The body is alive, but the system is weakened, and eventually is susceptible to limited and sluggish physical and mental abilities, to unhealthful and damaged body tissues, and to all sorts of illness.

You can weaken your enzyme potential by following an unhealthful diet. Just as a houseplant may display damage from a time that it was neglected, the body may also be damaged by a low quality diet. But, just as a plant can regain vigor when it is supplied with the right nutrients, so too can the human body.

The best way to prevent disease is to avoid doing things that help create the terrain for diseases to take hold. Following a vibrant diet consisting largely of raw fruits and vegetables is one major key to maintaining vibrant health.

Foods that damage enzymatic activity within the body include meat, milk, and eggs, and products made with them, which are all rich in free radicals. Enzyme damaging foods also includes fried and sautéed foods, and other foods containing highly heated oils, and foods that contain MSG, gluten grains, bleached foods, and artificial sweeteners, dyes, and flavorings, as well as other artificial ingredients. Eating these deadened foods clutters the system and puts the body out of tune with vibrant health.

The good news is that a system that has been damaged by unhealthful eating can be made healthier by cutting out deadened and deadening foods, and by eating a healthful, vibrant diet rich in raw fruits and vegetables. Because the biological factory that exists within the body is designed to function in a certain way, it will always work better if it is provided the proper fuel.

Your body cannot function at its highest level if you are not feeding it what it needs to function at that level. You can change that now, today, with your food choices. Make a conscious decision to select and eat food that is high quality, and preferably consisting of raw, organically grown fruits, vegetables, sprouts, herbs, nuts, seeds, and water plants.

Find the closest organic food co-op, or start one. Consider joining a CSA, which will supply a weekly box of fresh organic local produce. Where possible, plant and maintain a food garden. Plant native fruiting trees and bushes on your land, or nearby wild lands.

> "May the food we are eating make us aware of the interconnections between the universe and us, the earth and us, and all other living species and us. Because each bite contains in itself the life of the sun and the earth, may we see the meaning and value of life from these precious morsels of food."
> – Thich Nhat Hanh

FIBER

A diet rich in fiber is essential to vibrant health. Without a diet rich in fiber, your digestive tract does not function at its best.

Following a **low**-fiber diet increases your chances of experiencing hemorrhoids, varicose veins, vision problems, hiatal hernia, stroke, heart attack, and cancers, especially cancer of the colon and rectum.

> "Fiber, found only in plant foods, has many health-promoting qualities. It binds with carcinogens, fats, and cholesterol and eliminates them in the feces. By eliminating carcinogens, it reduces your risk of developing cancer, and by eliminating fat and cholesterol, it reduces your risk of heart disease, atherosclerosis, and obesity. Fiber also improves the efficiency of insulin, so that we need less of it to maintain appropriate blood-sugar levels."
> – Dr. John McDougall, author of *The Starch Solution*; DrMcDougall.com

Fiber helps to remove toxins from the system, reduces cholesterol, improves digestion, and helps maintain blood sugar levels.

Meat (including fish, birds, reptiles, and amphibians), dairy (milk and milk products: cheese, kefir, yogurt, cream, ice cream, sour cream, cream cheese, butter, whey, and casein), and eggs contain no fiber. Following a diet rich in these substances increases the chance of experiencing a variety of health problems, and especially if the dairy has been pasteurized and/or homogenized, and if the meat, dairy, and eggs are from animals raised on nonorganic farms. Meat, dairy, and eggs are rich in free radicals. As mentioned elsewhere in the book, cooking animal protein creates a variety of chemicals that also increase cancer risk, trigger autoimmune disorders, and play a role in other health maladies.

A low fat vegan diet is rich in fiber because fruits, vegetables, sprouts, nuts, seeds, and seaweeds all contain an abundance of fiber. A raw vegan diet that is especially rich in fruit and veggies is also rich in soluble fiber, which is beneficial in that it doesn't hold onto iron and some other nutrients like nonsoluble fiber. Both soluble and nonsoluble fiber, however, are beneficial to have in the diet.

While a nonvegan diet that is vegetarian may include milk products, including butter, ice cream, kefir, yogurt, and rennetless cheese, a vegan diet may contain nondairy, fiber-rich versions of these foods, including milk made from almonds, bananas, or hemp seeds; kefir made from coconut; ice cream made from frozen bananas; and vegan cheeses made of pine nuts, almonds, walnuts, sunflower seeds, or other nuts or seeds.

While some people concern themselves with getting enough fiber, and even try to calculate how much fiber they get at each meal – such as aiming for the suggested 14 grams of fiber for every 1,000 calories, I don't concern myself with those numbers. Because all I eat consists of plants, and all plants contain fiber, there is no way that I'm *not* getting enough fiber. It is the meat, dairy, and egg diet that lacks fiber – because, meat, dairy, and eggs don't contain fiber. A vegan diet rich in raw fruits and vegetables contains plenty of fiber, and there is no need for supplementing with fiber extracts, such as psyllium.

"There are many types of 'extracted' fiber products on the market, including tablets and powders that can be mixed with water and taken as a drink. Most health care professionals would advise a healthy adult to eat a pear or a handful of raisins instead of turning to a supplement. Satisfying your daily fiber needs with food is the best way to get a healthful balance of soluble and insoluble fiber.

It's also a great way to improve the overall quality of your diet, since fiber-rich foods tend to be rich in vitamins, minerals, and disease-fighting phytochemicals."

– Nancy D. Berkoff, RD, EdD, Ask the Nutritionist: How much fiber do I really need?; VegetarianTimes.com

Leaky Gut (damaged intestinal lining) Syndrome, Celiac, Crohn's, Irritable Bowel Syndrome, Intestinal Issues, Reflux, Heartburn, Gluten Intolerance, Candida, Skin Conditions, and Arthritis

A low-fat vegan diet rich in raw foods, and which may include steamed and boiled foods is beneficial for those with gluten, celiac, leaking gut, and arthritis and other rheumatoid and digestive issues. Especially if the person avoids gluten grains, corn, soy, bleached foods, processed sugars, MSG, and synthetic chemical food additives (colorings, flavorings, scents, and preservatives).

In his book *Prevent and Reverse Heart Disease*, Dr. Caldwell Esselstyn discourages the use of any bottled oils. So does Dr. John McDougall, author of *The Starch Solution.* Their advice is excellent not only for those who want to avoid heart disease while also lowering their risk of cancer and weight gain, but also for those with gluten, celiac, and leaky gut and digestive issues.

Soy and processed sugars can also be problematic for those with celiac. Esselstyn's diet includes soy. Both the diet encouraged in this book and that suggested by Esselstyn discourage the use of processed sugars. Esselstyn's book

39

provides recipes that contain very small amounts of sugar as an option. Both diets may or may not include maple syrup, depending on personal preference.

Leaky gut is a condition in which the larger molecules not being effectively broken down in the natural digestive processes taking place in the mouth, stomach, and intestines pass through the intestinal barrier – the intestinal mucosa – that has been damaged by bad foods, heated oils, animal protein, infectious agents (bacterial, protozoan, viral), pharmaceutical drugs (steroids, NSAIDS [nonsteroidal anti-inflammatory medications] cytotoxic drugs, and hormones including birth control pills), chemotherapy, radiation, and toxins. A depleted beneficial intestinal bacteria ("friendly flora") presence, such as from taking antibiotics, colloidal silver, antacid products, and from alcohol abuse, consuming processed sugars, and unhealthful diet can also play a role in leaking gut.

The larger molecules getting past the damaged intestinal barrier then enter into the bloodstream and act as antigens, which are foreign proteins, bacteria, and other substances that trigger immune system response. These antigens can play a role in autoimmune disorders, including certain types of arthritis and rheumatic diseases as the immune system develops autoantibodies that then attack the antigens.

While the liver can deal with some of the antigens, under the condition of leaky gut, the amount entering the bloodstream can overwhelm the liver, keeping the antigens in the bloodstream. They may then settle in the various tissues of the body, including connective tissues and muscles, where they can trigger inflammation. This is the body displaying activities of attacking its own tissues, and is labeled as "autoimmune disorder."

"Musculoskeletal complications are frequent and well-recognized manifestations in IBD (inflammatory bowel disease), and affect up to 33 percent of patients with IBD. The strong link between the bowel and the osteo-articular system is suggested by many clinical and experimental observations."

– Rheumatic Manifestations of Inflammatory Bowel Disease; *World Journal of Gastroenterology*, Nov. 28, 2009

People with inflammatory arthritis are often found to have inflammation of the intestinal walls. They are often given pharmaceutical drugs that are known to damage the intestinal walls, including by forming ulcers, making the patient's condition chronically worse. The patient may also be treated with immunosuppression drugs that can damage health. The patient also might take common over-the-counter anti-inflammatory drugs, which damage the intestines, increasing permeability, which is "leaky gut syndrome," which increases the passage of antigens and bacteria into the blood, and that increases the possibility of arthritis, kidney disease, vision degeneration, and damage to other areas rich in the smaller blood passageways, the capillaries. The drugs can also increase the possibility of other health problems, including osteoporosis – leading people to reason that they need to increase their calcium and vitamin D intake, and this may lead them to drinking more milk with the belief that milk contains what they need. Increasing their milk intake will only magnify their health problems, increasing the risk of leaky gut, arthritis, and osteoporosis… and macular degenerations, lupus, and kidney disease, and cancer.

Sufferers of rheumatic diseases would benefit by cleaning up their diet, including by eliminating all animal protein from their food choices.

People with other inflammatory conditions, including tendinitis, periostitis, and granulomatous bone and joint lesions, also benefit from a low-fat vegan diet containing absolutely no heated oils, but that is rich in raw fruits and vegetables. They may then experience a halt to the immunopathogenesis of their ailment. This is especially so if the low-fat vegan diet is geared toward alkaline foods, such as including green vegetables, but staying away from gluten and bleached grains. Taking a vegan probiotic supplement, on top of following a vegan diet, aids in the healing of the intestines.

"The largest amount of lymphoid tissue in the body is associated with the gut. This tissue protects the body from antigens that do get through the intestinal barrier. Unfortunately, an unhealthy diet – too high in fat, cholesterol, and animal protein – can compromise the capacities of the lymphoid tissue to destroy invading antigens that make it through the intestinal wall.

Fasting is known to decrease intestinal permeability, thus making the gut 'less leaky.' This may be one of the reasons fasting has been shown to dramatically benefit patients with rheumatoid arthritis. When patients return after the fast to a diet with dairy products, the gut becomes more permeable and the arthritis returns."

– Diet: Only Hope for Arthritis, by Dr. John McDougall, author of *The Starch Solution*; DrMcDougall.com. Anyone suffering from leaky gut, lupus, arthritis, and other similar health issues would benefit by reading McDougall's book and following a low-fat vegan diet.

I had a friend who was diagnosed with an ulcer. Her doctor told her to drink milk and he put her on prescription anti-inflammatory drugs. What his reasoning was escapes me, other than he was stuck in antiquated concepts and believing in misinformation he gleaned from medical schooling controlled by the pharmaceutical industry.

A person with intestinal issues, and especially with a damaged intestinal mucosa, should not be consuming animal products, in particular any sort of dairy. Anti-inflammatory drugs carry the side effect of causing intestinal damage. Consuming animal protein and taking drugs that increase the possibility of damaging the intestinal walls when the intestinal walls are already damaged increases the possibility of undigested macroproteins and bacteria passing through the intestinal walls and entering into the bloodstream. The antigens then would be attacked by the immune system. The entire scenario increases the likelihood of an autoimmune disorder diagnosis – for which pharmacology medications would be prescribed.

By understanding the situation that can lead to inflammatory arthritis, it should be no surprise that so many sports stars end up with arthritis. They spend years eating high-protein diets and taking anti-inflammatory drugs and painkillers. It is the perfect scenario for triggering their chronic and degenerative health conditions.

The low-fat vegan diet advocated in this book specifically encourages alkaline foods rich in omega-3 fatty acids, which are important for those experiencing inflammatory ailments, including celiac, leaking gut, ulcers, tendinitis, and arthritis. While there are omega-3-rich foods in all raw fruits and vegetables, they are especially rich in raw green leafed vegetables, raw hemp seeds; sprouts, such as sunflower sprouts; and germinates, such as germinated quinoa, chia, and buckwheat.

This book discourages following a diet rich in omega-6 fatty acids, which can be problematic for those with celiac, gluten intolerance, leaking gut, arthritis, and other inflammatory diseases. Omega-6 fatty acids are more present in packaged and processed foods, and in bottled oils, such as canola, safflower, corn, and sunflower oils. For better health, simply avoid all heated oils (including fried foods and sautéed foods) and all bottled oils, including olive oil, flax oil, sesame oil, sunflower oil, canola oil, corn oil, and other oils. A low-fat diet containing no added oils is best. If you do use oils, use them sparingly and stick with raw organic coconut oil and hemp seed oil (store them in the refrigerator or freezer).

You got used to a diet containing all of the substances that cause health problems. Now, get used to a diet that eliminates those damaging substances, but encourages the use of foods that infuse vibrant health.

If you have had issues with leaky gut syndrome, inflammatory arthritis, juvenile idiopathic arthritis, joint pain, spondylarthritis, spondyloarthropathies, ulcers, celiac, gluten sensitivity, colitis, reflux, heartburn, indigestion, inflammatory bowel disease, kidney disorders, urinary tract infections, food allergies, food sensitivities, acne, eczema, psoriasis, dermatitis, rashes, hives, hepatitis, pancreatitis, asthma, fibromyalgia, MS, lupus, HIV infection, alcoholism, fatigue, anxiety, or schizophrenia, you will likely find a favorable response to following a gluten-free, low-fat vegan diet rich in raw fruits and vegetables, and free of soy, processed sugars, synthetic chemicals, and fried or sautéed oils, and foods that have been fried, roasted, broiled, toasted, grilled, or microwaved. If cooked foods are desired, go for oil-free steamed veggies or boiled foods (such as no-oil vegan soups, vegan chili, legumes, quinoa, wild rice, millet, oats, etc.).

(Note that I did not say the diet can cure those conditions; however, many people have found that following the type of diet advocated in this book cleared their body of or greatly reduced the symptoms of many ailments.)

If citrus, strawberries, certain nuts, and vegetables like carrots and beets tend to cause irritation or upset, also avoid those. Nightshades, like tomatoes, potatoes, peppers, eggplant, paprika, and pimentos may only be eaten if they are thoroughly cooked, or avoided altogether – and reintroduced into the diet months later to see how the person reacts. Those with sensitivity to almonds may find that getting truly raw almonds and soaking them overnight will relieve that issue.

One way of damaging the digestive tract is by following a diet that is low in fiber. Low fiber diets are found to increase permeability of the intestinal tract, which is not good. High fiber diets decrease the permeability, which is good. Meat, dairy, and eggs do not contain fiber. Plant matter contains fiber. By eliminating the nonfiber items while increasing the fiber in the diet, the digestive tract will function better. As mentioned elsewhere in the book, a diet rich in fiber is also beneficial for cardiovascular and brain health. The diet advocated in this book is rich both in soluble and insoluble fiber.

You may also benefit by adding vegan probiotics to your foods, or taking a vegan probiotic supplement. An unhealthful diet of junk foods, processed sugars, bottled oils, and bleached grains may have brought about the presence of harmful intestinal bacteria, including candida, citrobacter, clostridium difficile (also known as C.diff, and which can cause chronic and severe diarrhea), and hafnia. These bacteria can contribute to leaky gut syndrome and interfere with both nutrient production and nutrient absorption. Following a gluten-free, low-fat vegan diet while also taking a vegan probiotic supplement can eliminate the dysbiosis (bacterial imbalance) and restore balance to the intestinal flora, helping to heal the digestive tract. Beneficial strains of bacteria include Bifidobacterium, Lactobacillus, and Saccharomyces boulardii.

Because beneficial intestinal bacteria are necessary for the immune system to function, a healthful digestive tract will result in a stronger immune system. Not only will a clean diet improve the immune system, but also other systems and organs will function better, including the liver, bile ducts, pancreas, and kidneys, as they will have fewer toxins flowing through them.

Under conditions of leaky gut, the liver is continually being taxed by having to remove oxidized enteric toxins and macromolecules (the larger molecules that are able to pass through a damaged intestinal barrier). This can worsen the conditions of those with hepatitis and other liver issues.

Because so many beneficial molecules, including those relating to our emotions, are formed in the intestinal tract, following the diet advocated in this book will also likely improve mood and sleep while decreasing stress, anxiety, and irritability.

The intestinal lining can heal rather quickly. People switching to a clean diet free of bleached foods, gluten grains, fried and sautéed foods, clarified oils, animal protein, processed sugars and salts, and synthetic chemicals, but rich in truly raw fruits and vegetables often find that they feel much better within one to two weeks of following the diet. Be sure to chew your foods. That is part of the digestive process as the salivary glands excrete substances that start the breakdown of the materials you eat. Saliva also contains epidermal growth factor (EGF), a polypeptide found to play a role in the growth of the epithelial cells lining the digestive tract. EGF is particularly important to the replacement of the cells lining the tract, which continually slough off and regenerate. You may have heard the saying, "Chew your juices and drink your solids." In other words, don't gulp your juices or smoothies so fast. Slow down and savor them. Chew your solid food.

STEPS TOWARD BETTER DIGESTION AND NUTRITION: SOAKING AND ACTIVATING NUTS, SEEDS, BEANS, AND GRAINS

SUBSTANCES called antinutrients, including tannins, lectins, phytates, and complex sugars are contained in seeds, beans, nuts, and grains. They are called antinutrients because they can interfere with nutrient absorption, inhibit digestive enzymes, alter the ability of the digestive system to break down certain substances, impact the function of the pancreas, play some role in autoimmune and allergic reactions, and may contribute to degenerative and chronic health conditions, such as bone loss and joint pain.

A person may say that they have been eating seeds, beans, nuts, and grains their entire life, and they are fine. Of course, but you can also likely improve your nutrition. Maybe some of the health problems you have experienced, including allergies, stomach upset, stress injuries, sleep disorders, and other maladies were related to what you may have consumed in common foods. Some of the antinutrients are destroyed by heat, which is why you may not have experienced their effects. This chapter isn't about saying you are going to get sick, it is simply about improving nutrition. It is also about getting more live foods in your diet, helping you to get the most out of your foods, and providing ways to be more likely to experience vibrant health.

Some of the antinutrients are part of the defense mechanism to protect the seed, bean, grain, or nut from fungi, bacteria, viruses, insects, and exposure to sun radiation and extreme temperatures. The presence of these defensive substances is why seeds can last many years and remain viable. When the conditions are right, with the temperatures and moisture ideal for the seed to sprout, certain inhibitors are no longer needed, the coat or skin of protection will fall from or peel from the seed, or become a nutrient base, enzymes will come into play, and the seed will germinate and sprout.

Enzyme inhibitors in nuts, seeds, beans, and grains can interfere with digestive enzymes and other enzymes in our system. While heat can destroy some of these substances, the enzyme inhibitors are also neutralized by soaking raw, unheated nuts, seeds, beans, and grains before use. Soaking breaks down complex sugars, phytates, tannins, and other antinutrient components, and triggers the production of beneficial enzymes rich in the amino acids we need for protein, and makes nuts, seeds, beans, and grains more digestible and nutritious. As explained below, fermenting can also help disable, disband, or otherwise neutralize certain antinutrients.

Trypsin, an enzyme important in the digestion of protein, is one that has been identified as being affected by enzyme inhibitors in foods. Diets rich in trypsin inhibitors alter the function of the pancreas, leading to hypersecretion of pancreatic enzymes. This can inflame the pancreas and interfere with insulin resistance, alter the immune system, and make the person more susceptible to allergy issues.

Those with health issues relating to blood sugar balance, digestive upset, allergies, or problems related to pancreatic function would benefit by only consuming raw nuts, beans, seeds, and grains that have been activated through soaking and/or fermenting.

Those with a history of anorexia or bulimia, reflux, heartburn, food allergies, skin disorders, acne, arthritis, osteoporosis, bloating, leaking gut syndrome, or irritable bowel syndrome may find that they do much better on a diet of activated nuts, seeds, beans, and fermented nongluten grains, in combination with a low-fat diet that is rich in raw fruits and vegetables.

Phytate or phytic acid is a naturally occurring protective substance bound with phosphorus in nuts, beans, seeds, and grains and prevents the embryo of the seed from damage. Phytates can interfere with nutrient absorption, including of certain minerals such as calcium, copper, iron, magnesium, and zinc. One enzyme that is produced when seeds germinate is phytase, which neutralizes phytic acid. This is why it is good to soak nuts, beans, and seeds before consuming, including before boiling beans. It is also why it is good to soak and/or ferment grains before consuming. Be sure to toss away the soak water.

For all of the above reasons, those raw vegans calling themselves "living foodists" aim to consume only raw, soaked, germinated, "activated" nuts and seeds, in addition to raw fruits and vegetables, sprouts, and seaweeds, and foods consisting only of those ingredients.

Whether it is pumpkin seeds, sunflower seeds, chia seeds, garbanzo beans (chickpeas), black beans, hazelnuts, walnuts, almonds, pine nuts (pignolis), or other nuts, seeds, or beans, there is nutritional benefit in getting them raw, unheated, unpasteurized, and viable, and activating them before consumption. Certain ones, including nuts, pumpkin seeds, and beans can then be dried for using in coming weeks, such as by placing the activated nuts, seeds, and beans in a dehydrator at low temperature, and then storing them for use in coming weeks. Some natural foods stores sell activated seeds and nuts that have been dried. It is best to store them in a cool, dry place, or in a refrigerator.

You may benefit by learning about fermented foods made of activated seeds and/or activated nuts, including activated, fermented, raw vegan seed and nut cheeses. These are rich in a variety of nutrients, including probiotics – especially if vegan probiotics were used as one of the ingredients.

Primates don't typically consume seeds or legumes, and humans appear to have only done so at an increasing rate mostly with the start of agricultural practices that grew over thousands of years into modern-day crop farming techniques. One reason for the lack of seeds or grains in the human diet previous to about 10,000 or so years ago is that they are too hard to eat unless they are soaked, or made into a powder, and/or boiled or roasted. Even today there are those who avoid eating nuts, beans, and seeds, and they find that their health is perfectly fine on a diet consisting of some combination of fruits, vegetables, and sprouts, including in juices, smoothies, salads, and other concoctions.

Ancient peoples may not have known about the reactions that could result when eating unsoaked grains, beans, seeds, and nuts. One reason they soaked them is that it makes them makes them easier to chew, and because soaking makes them softer, which meant they didn't have to use as much fuel to cook them into a softer, more easily chewed condition. They didn't know that the soaking and fermenting also helped to deactivate and break down what we now call antinutrients, including phytates, complex sugars, tannins, certain enzyme inhibitors, and so forth.

Activating raw nuts, seeds, and beans by soaking them makes them more nutrient dense. Soaking also makes the nutrients more bioavailable and triggers the nuts, beans, and seeds to begin producing the nutrients, including antioxidants, vitamins, and amino acids needed for the seed to grow into a plant.

Use glass, ceramic, or stone containers for soaking, not plastic or metal.

Hard beans, including adzuki, black beans, kidney beans, mung, navy beans, and pinto beans, contain complex sugars called oligosaccharides which are not broken down by the digestive system. Instead, oligosaccharides can ferment in the digestive tract, resulting in gas. This is another reason why it is good to get your beans raw and soak them in water for a day before boiling. Be sure to dispose of the soak water – do not use it to boil the beans, and do not use it in recipes.

People often make lentils and split peas without soaking them for at least several hours, or overnight. Just like other legumes, it is good to activate lentils and split peas before using.

Some people use a little salt in the soak water when soaking legumes as salt helps to disable the enzyme inhibitors. Others say you should skip the salt, instead adding a little apple cider vinegar or freshly squeezed lemon juice to the soak water. Changing the water after several hours can help in the activation process. Experiment and learn for yourself.

When soaking raw nuts, including almonds, Brazil nuts, hazelnuts, macadamia, pecans, pine nuts, pistachio, and walnuts, and also seeds like pumpkin, fenugreek, and sesame, use one-quarter teaspoon of natural, unprocessed sea salt, pink salt, or other natural salt in the water per cup of nuts or seeds. (Cashews are not truly raw, even if they are marketed as "raw," and there is no need to soak or activate them. Living foodists don't use cashews.) The Aztecs traditionally soaked pumpkin seeds in salt water. After several hours you may want to strain the water and add more and let them soak for another several hours. When done soaking, strain and spread out on a ceramic platter and put them in a barely warm oven, or in the sun, or on a dehydrator sheet and dehydrate on low heat to fully dry.

Make sure activated seeds and nuts are well dried if you are going to store them, and keep them in a sealed container in the refrigerator or other cold storage.

Many people don't think of coconuts as nuts, but they are. Like other nuts, coconuts contain phytic acid – however, they contain lower amounts than other nuts. The phytate content in coconut is why some living foodists will ferment coconut meat into raw vegan yogurt overnight by blending or mashing the coconut meat with vegan probiotics. People who have had stomach or intestinal upset often find this fermented coconut yogurt to be very soothing to their system.

The phytate content in coconut is one reason why people who are otherwise raw foodists may eat coconut that has been heated or steamed, which are processes that can destroy the phytates. Young coconut meat is somewhat liquid, and would need to be heated in a double boiler. The harder coconut meat can be steamed in a vegetable steamer.

I don't typically eat heated coconut. I do sometimes have fermented coconut yogurt.

Those who consume raw coconut and raw chocolate together are getting a strong dose of phytates, and this may contribute to skin outbreaks as both coconut and chocolate contain phytates.

Chia seeds, flax seeds, and buckwheat can quickly become mucilaginous when soaking, so it is a bit difficult to strain them. Chia seeds quickly germinate, and are pretty much impossible to dry out, so they need to be used within minutes, hours, or a day or so of soaking. Flax seeds that are wet tend to stick solidly to anything and need to be used in recipes soon after soaking, but they can be dried in a dehydrator or through other drying means. Buckwheat can be strained and rinsed in a mesh strainer and kept in the fridge for use within coming days, and can also be dried, such as in a dehydrator.

If kidney beans get beyond the activated stage, and turn into germinates – with a stem, or a sprout (with leaves), they should not be eaten as they can make you sick, very sick. Hemoagglutinins are substances that cause the agglutination of red blood cells and also interfere with cellular metabolism processes. Small doses of ricin, the toxic hemmagglutinin lectin extract of the castor bean, can kill a human.

Phytohemagglutinins in germinated or sprouted adzuki beans, black beans, blackeyed peas, lentils, lima beans, peas, and white butter beans can be problematic. Red kidney beans have been identified as having the highest amount of hemagglutinins. In other words, hemagglutinins are toxic. Because cooking destroys the hemagglutinins, these foods should be consumed only in a well-boiled or thoroughly steamed stage.

If you purchase bean powders, "instant beans," and "instant falafel" products that you add water to before eating, and other such processed and "instant" foods, you may want to consider how you feel after consuming them. If you experience digestive upset, the beans may not have been cooked thoroughly enough to rid them of hemagglutinins. I discourage people from using such products, and also discourage them from eating canned beans – which may not have been thoroughly cooked (and can contain a variety of toxins leached from the lining of the can).

You may say that you consume germinated or sprouted lentils all the time in your salad. Well, pay attention and consider how you feel after eating soaked, germinated, or sprouted lentils. If you feel that they are making you ill, discontinue eating them raw. Hemmaggluttinin poisoning may include digestive upset, cramping, abdominal pain, headache, nausea, and diarrhea. You may want to stick to well-boiled lentils.

Amaranth, brown rice, buckwheat, millet, quinoa, wild rice, and steel cut oats can all be soaked for several hours before use in various recipes, including those for breakfast cereals, granola, and pie crusts. Rinse them in a screen strainer before soaking. It can also be helpful to add a little bit (a tablespoon per cup of grain) of an acidic ingredient to the soaking water, such as apple cider vinegar or freshly squeezed lemon or lime juice. Do not use salt when soaking grains. After soaking for several hours or overnight, strain out the soak water.

Raw grain flours can also be mixed with water several hours before use. Obviously, flours can't be strained. Simply then use the wet flour in recipes. Those who do soak their flours have found that the subsequent food is lighter, fluffier, and tastes better.

Living foodists who eat activated corn or activated corn meal use corn or corn meal that has been soaked in "lime water." Lime water is not lime juice. Lime juice is from squeezed lime fruit. Lime water is made by putting dolomite powder into a canning jar filled with water, stirring it, and leaving it to sit for several hours to let the powder settle, then carefully pouring out the water without stirring the settled powder. Use a tablespoon of lime water per cup of raw corn for soaking corn or corn meal for several hours or overnight. Strain out the water, then add vegan probiotics and let sit for several hours in the refrigerator before using the corn in recipes, such as for polenta. This activated corn can go rancid if it isn't kept refrigerated or frozen.

I discourage people from eating bread, but if they do choose to eat bread they can make healthier choices, including staying away from commercially processed junk breads made with low quality ingredients and unfermented gluten grains. If you do choose to eat bread, seek out truly fermented sourdough bread. Most "sourdough" bread on the market is low quality garbage bread that was not made using the ancient practice of fermenting the grain. Commercial bread often also contains unnatural substances and garbage oils.

Read up about how sourdough bread is made in a traditional manner, by fermenting the grains. The fermenting process and soaking gluten grains (wheat, rye, barley, bulgur, durum, kamut, semolina, spelt, triticale) can help to break down gluten. But there may still be some reaction by people sensitive to gluten. There are ways of using nongluten grains to make sourdough bread so that there is no concern about reactions to gluten.

DEHYDRATED FOODS

DEHYDRATED foods in sunfood cuisine include common dehydrated foods like raisins, dried tomatoes, dried figs, and prunes. They also include dehydrated, but not cooked or high-temperature heated, dessert crusts; dehydrated flat breads; dehydrated chips; dehydrated sweet cookies; dehydrated veggie burgers; dehydrated pizza crusts; dehydrated seed and vegetable crackers; kale chips; and also dehydrated granola mixes made of germinated seeds and soaked nuts.

I don't eat many dehydrated foods. If I do make them, it is usually dehydrated seed and veggie crackers using flax seeds mixed with fresh pulp left over from juicing vegetables. One reason I don't make dehydrated pine nut cheese is because I will devour as much of that stuff as I can get my hands on!

Dehydrating food is a way to create foods that can be stored for lengthy periods – such as for emergency food storage. They also provide foods that can be taken on trips so that you don't have to depend on lower-quality foods.

It is good to eat dehydrated foods along with those that are in their fresh state, such as by spreading guacamole, or raw vegan pâtés or sauces on dehydrated seed and vegetable crackers. With raw pizza, the crust is dehydrated, but the topping consists of a variety of regular but uncooked and thinly sliced toppings, as well as raw vegan pesto sauce. Dehydrated pine nut cheeses can be used in green salads, or pine nut cheese that has not been dehydrated can be used as a spread on dehydrated vegetable and seed crackers. Dehydrated sweet breads (made of diced fruit and soaked oats, for instance) can be eaten with raw vegan berry cream sauces (berries blended with soaked nuts, dates, and cinnamon).

If you eat too many dehydrated foods, you may end up feeling dehydrated. Water or other fluid, such as vegetable juice, or lemon-infused rejuvelac, are good to drink with dehydrated foods, otherwise, you may experience rough digestion and flatulence if you eat too much dehydrated food by itself.

Dehydrated foods are made using low heat to preserve the nutrients, and especially the enzymes, of the living plant substances.

There are many figures thrown around as to what is the maximum temperature to use when dehydrating foods without damaging the nutrients. Various raw vegan recipe books state that the figure is 105° F, and others say it is 120° F – or 118° F. How they came up with these figures is anyone's guess. The temperature at which the enzymes are damaged depends on which plant substance you are dehydrating.

As an experiment I put flax seeds, sunflower seeds, and pumpkin seeds in a 125° F dehydrator, then I took the seeds and kept them moist. They sprouted.

While 125° F may not harm some seeds, including those that survive through forest fires and desert heat, that temperature is probably too high to use when dehydrating things like fruits and vegetables and their pulp. As I mentioned, I don't use the dehydrator much, and I don't eat many dehydrated foods, but when I do, I use a lower temperature, about 110° F, for those types of foods.

Ideally, dehydrating will remove only the water from the food you are dehydrating, while preserving nutrients. What is left over is a much smaller piece of food with an intensified flavor.

The first time I ate gourmet raw vegan pizza crust I was convinced that dehydrated foods were something to look into. It was made by Jeremy Safron, and he had brought it with him from Hawaii as he was passing through Southern California. His recipe book *The Raw Truth: The Art of Preparing Living Foods* contains a recipe for raw pizza. (If you are seeking a gourmet raw recipe book, Jeremy's *The Raw Truth* is easily one of the better ones.)

Those who are used to eating cooked food may need to adjust their expectations of what crackers, flat breads, and cookies will taste like when they first take a bite out of those that are made using low-heat dehydrators. Some foods may taste very familiar, while others may provide a new taste experience, and others may not be desirable.

As in any other type of food, there are dehydrated foods that are satisfying, and others that you may not enjoy so much. The key is to explore and find the ones that work for you. I have found some I like, and some I'd rather never taste ever again. On the occasion that I go to raw restaurants, I usually avoid their dehydrated foods, but not always.

If you are used to eating cooked foods, you may find that the density of dehydrated foods will satisfy that feeling of fullness that you are used to. But it is good not to rely so much on dehydrated foods, and to make your diet consist largely of fresh foods, such as fresh fruit, salads rich in a variety of fresh fruits and vegetables, and some homemade green smoothies. It is always better if you can grow some of your foods.

To increase the nutritional quality of the nuts and seeds you may be using in such things as dehydrated crackers, crusts, biscotti, cookies, and crusts, soak the nuts or seeds in water for several hours, then rinse and let them germinate for a day. This will trigger the nutrient-making machinery in the nuts and seeds, providing more enzymes, amino acids, essential fatty acids, biophotons, and other nutrients that are less present in unsprouted nuts and seeds.

You can dehydrate any food, from fruits and vegetables to herbs and edible flowers to sea vegetables and germinates or sprouts.

There are many dehydrators on the market, but the oldest tool for dehydrating foods is one that has been used since the earliest of times. That tool is called sun.

Ancient people, and some even today, prepare dehydrated foods using sun by laying them on top of such things as rocks, adobe bricks, dried tree bark or wood, or on ceramic flats or plates.

Someone I know dehydrates foods using a shallow box he made of wood, with a ceramic plate at the bottom. A suspended screen in the center acts as a shelf to put the food on. A screened lid keeps out bugs.

When dehydrating foods using sun, you need to learn to prevent the food from baking, as a base of a ceramic plate can get quite hot when sun is at or near the day's zenith.

By checking the community board of your local natural foods store, or online, you may be able to find people selling used dehydrators.

Because each type of fruit and vegetable, and the various types of raw recipes for dehydrated foods, contain different amounts of water, some foods take longer to dehydrate than others. The room temperature plays a big part in how long it takes to dehydrate a food. But it is best to dehydrate the foods at low temperatures so that the nutrients, such as the essential fatty acids, are not damaged. Simply leave in a dehydrator until the desired level of dryness is reached, then store in a sealed container in a cool, dry place.

Many of the raw vegan recipe books contain recipes for dehydrated foods. Check out *Living Cuisine: The Art and Spirit of Raw Foods*, by Renée Loux.

SEA VEGETABLES

SEA vegetables are the thallus, or body; the lamina, leaves, ribbons, or blades; the stems or stipe; the sorus or clusters; haptera, or finger-like extensions; and the bulbs, air bladder, or floats of the Protista Kingdom life-forms. They are algae, and are not considered to be true plants. This is why some people say that sea vegetables are not vegetables. But if you call them "sea vegetables," people will know what you are speaking of – even when you are meaning "algae," which aren't true plants.

Got that? If not, don't lose any sleep over it. If someone tries to get technical with you on this issue, pretend you don't hear them. The conversation can go easier that way.

Unlike plants, seaweeds lack reproductive mechanisms in the form of flowers or cones. They also do not contain the vascular systems that exist in plants, from which nutrients are taken in through roots and transported to other areas of the distant structure – the branches and the leaves. Instead, seaweeds absorb nutrients directly from being in contact with water, and through their interaction with sunlight photons. Seaweeds do feature structural forms resembling vascular mechanisms, but these are the stipe, which are basically the spines that support the structure.

There are over 9,000 species of seaweed and they grow at or near the surface of water. The gas-containing bulbs, air bladders, or floats and other gas-containing compartments of seaweeds help them to float, improving their ability to absorb sunlight photons, which they convert into energy for the plant to use and store.

Like plants, seaweeds do conduct photosynthesis and feature varieties of light-absorbing pigments.

In other words, seaweeds contain bountiful nutrients and spectrums of light drawn in from the ocean and sun.

There are several types of chlorophyll, and each has a slightly different molecular structure and photosynthesis process. The most common type of chlorophyll is chlorophyll-a, which is found in all plants, in seaweeds, and also in blue-green algae, which is cyanobacteria.

Although they all contain the green pigment of chlorophyll, the color of the seaweed can be anywhere from brown to green to red. The color depends on the variety of seaweed, and on what level of the spectrum of light they were exposed to while growing.

Seaweeds are considered a sustainable food because they grow swiftly, including some that grow two or more feet per day, don't require land, require no manageable resources, and don't create land erosion. Seaweeds also absorb carbon dioxide and produce oxygen.

Many types of seaweed are not edible, or perhaps have a taste that humans don't appreciate.

Many people don't know that they have been consuming and using products containing seaweed. Extracts of kelp, including texturing agents known as agar, alginate, and carrageenan, have been used in the food industry to thicken chocolate milk, to provide creaminess to some brands of yogurt and cheese, to create dietary supplements, and even to make beer foamier. Some types of farm animal feed also contain seaweed. Seaweed and seaweed extracts are also used in cosmetics, toothpaste, skin lotions, and haircare products. Potash used in gunpowder comes from kelp.

You may find water vegetables under the following names: agar agar, arame, chlorella, dulse, focus tip (also named bladderwrack), grapestone, kelp (there are hundreds of varieties of kelp), kombu, Nori (also known as mei bil, sea leaf, and porphyra), ocean ribbons, sea lettuce, sea palm, silky sea palm, sea whip, wakame, spirulina, and wild blue-green algae (Aphanizomenon flos aqua).

Not surprisingly, sea vegetables consist mostly of water. When dried, they can have shrunk to less than 1/20 of their original size.

Sea vegetables are a source of the element iodine, which is fundamental to thyroid and brain function, metabolism, hormone production, and stress reduction. In addition to chlorophyll, nutrients in water vegetables include amino acids, essential fatty acids, peptides, enzymes, biophotons, and vitamins A, C, D, E, and K; a variety of minerals; betacarotene and other antioxidants, and folic acid and other B vitamins.

Eating water vegetables provides nutrients that decrease the chances of experiencing a variety of ailments, and also that help to regenerate cells, build the immune system, detoxify body tissues, and aid in the absorption and utilization of nutrients. They also assist in the removal of heavy metals from the body; aid in the regulation of cholesterol; reduce cramps and anemia; alkalize the digestive tract and body tissues; regulate the thyroid; restore endocrine deficiencies; improve antibody production; balance the hormones and insulin; improve kidney and adrenal processes; and provide for better neural function. Sea vegetables contain a wider variety of bioavailable minerals than any other class of food.

The colloidal carbohydrate, alginic acid (sodium alginates), found in brown algae, binds with the heavy metals cadmium, lead, and mercury, as well as low-level radioactive material, and removes them from the body.

The calcium and iron in sea vegetables is more bioavailable to the human body than the same nutrients found in animal meat or milk. This is because animal products bring in substances that reduce and can decrease absorption of certain nutrients. Seaweeds are far superior sources of minerals, and contain more nutrients than milk, meat, and eggs.

Raw and low-temperature dried water vegetables contain healthful doses of enzymes. Out of the variety of sea vegetables, dulse contains the highest amount of the mineral manganese, which triggers the body to release more enzymes, improving digestion. Pinches of dulse can be added to a variety of foods, including juices, smoothies, salads, hummus, cilantro pesto, and vegetable pâté.

Another benefit of sea vegetables is that, like mushrooms, they contain glyconutrients, which are bitter carbohydrates. Our bodies use these long-chain sugars as energy and they also improve both tissue elasticity and the immune system. Some companies are trying to sell glyconutrient supplements as if they are some new, world-changing substance. But you don't have to purchase high priced, corporatized and commercialized glyconutrient supplement pills to get glyconutrients. By eating a variety of seaweeds you will obtain all of the glyconutrients that have been identified. You also don't need to consume hordes of sea vegetables to benefit from their glyconutrient content. Using a little seaweed here and there in your diet, such as kelp or dulse powder in salad dressings and, if you make them, in green smoothies, and adding dulse, kelp, or wakame to salads, will supply adequate amounts of glyconutrients and the other beneficial substances in sea vegetables. The raw green powder products, such as Infinity Greens and VitaMineral Green available at natural foods stores, contain a variety of aquatic vegetables.

The freshwater algae, chlorella, helps to remove toxins from the body. The porphyrins and sporopollenim in chlorella bind with heavy metals in the blood traveling in the walls of the intestines, removing the heavy metals from the system. Chlorella is also beneficial because it is rich in amino acids, chlorophyll, beta-carotene, B-6, and the healthful minerals iron, magnesium, phosphorus, and potassium. The alpha- and gamma-linoleic acid lipids (essential fatty acids) in chlorella help to transfer nutrients into the tissues, and are excellent for brain health. Chlorella is an excellent substance to include in your daily diet if you are detoxifying from substance abuse, including tobacco use.

Learn about ways of incorporating seaweeds into your diet.

Don't be surprised if you find yourself being corrected by someone who hears you call seaweeds "vegetables" or "plants" by saying that seaweeds are algae, and are not true plants. They may even say that "seaweed" is a colloquial term not definitive of any specific form. This situation is similar to that of the way some people refer to mushrooms as "vegetables." Mushrooms are also not plants, but are fungi. Oh, and, of course, blue-green algae are cyanobacteria, and commonly called *algae*, not a *seaweed*. And, tomatoes, avocados, and cucumbers are fruits, not vegetables.

WILD FOODS

"What is a weed? A plant whose virtues have not yet been discovered."
— Ralph Waldo Emerson

"We would be better off nutritionally if we threw away the crops we so laboriously raise in our fields and gardens and ate the weeds that grow with no encouragement from us."
— Euell Gibbons, *Stalking the Healthful Herbs*

ONE way to avoid eating unnatural foods, such as those that are grown using toxic chemicals, or that have been genetically altered, is to eat wild foods. These are foods that grow in the wild, such as various herbs, greens, fruits, vegetables, berries, flowers, and other edible plant substances, such as sea vegetables (arame, dulse, kombu [kelp], nori, and sea palm). Some of these are more nutritional than some items you will find in your local market produce section.

Eating the wild, natural plants from your region is good for the body because wild plants carry a strong electric charge and hold nutrients that are what you need for the region where you live. In other words, eating wild foods from your region connects you to nature as it adjusts your system and energy frequency to your environment. Eating the wild plants from your region can also help alleviate seasonal allergies.

Those who advocate raw honey often mention that eating local honey can help alleviate seasonal allergies. However, many people also are opposed to honey consumption, as they believe the honey the bees store is for their own use, and should not be stolen from them.

65

For most of the history of humanity, the plants people ate consisted of those growing in their region of the world, and much of that consisted of what they foraged on day hikes, including plants they had nurtured. Even when our ancestors began growing plants from other areas, they would eat them only after they were grown in their region. If they didn't have greenhouses, they could only grow and eat plant substances that survived in their region, and only in the season in which they grew.

Everything changed with refrigeration; with the creation of large greenhouses heated by electricity or gas; and with the invention of the engines that allow for shipping food to distant lands.

Today not only do people not eat wild foods from their region, they often subsist on diets that mostly consist of foods grown in other regions of the world, and foods grown using chemicals.

Except for a few years of unhealthful eating, one thing that I have enjoyed throughout my life is not only growing some of my own food and sharing it with others, but also discovering the edible plants that grow in the regions where I have lived. From my earliest childhood I was able to locate wild berry bushes, fruit trees, and vegetables. I have found food plants in some of the most unlikely areas.

Where I grew up there were many apple, cherry, plum, pear, and peach trees growing in the woods and fields. These, along with wild tomatoes, grapes, and berries provided many meals for me as I spent time outside in the late spring, summer, and early fall. Climbing a tree to reach the fruit at the top is one way to connect with nature.

When I was a small boy I made friends with various hoboes and random travelers who would camp in the woods along the nearby railroad tracks. Maybe some were running from the law, some were dodging the draft, and some had gone through terrible life situations. But, they always appreciated knowing where they could get free fruit. I realized early that some adults don't recognize some of the most common food plants.

A growing number of people never harvest their own food. Recently, I offered a neighbor some of the vegetables from my garden. She said she doesn't eat stuff like that, "out of the dirt." I asked her what she ate. She said, "What they sell at the store." Oh.

The more hardy seeds will survive to grow, blossom, and fruit in the wild – where they are not treated with chemicals. Because they are not treated with fertilizers, the roots of wild fruit and nut trees and wild fruit vines and berry bushes will often grow deeper into the ground to reach for nutrients. This results in fruits and berries that have a higher mineral content, are naturally balanced, are more vibrant, and carry a stronger frequency than fruit and vegetables grown using chemicals.

If you see fruit or other wild food growing on private land, contact the owner and see if he or she will allow you to harvest some of it.

Find out which food plants are native to your region, and plant and nurture some of these.

Fallen Fruit, FallenFruit.org. Fruit share site.
Food Not Lawns, FoodNotLawns.com
Food Routes, FoodRoutes.org
Kitchen Gardeners, KitchenGardeners.org
Local Harvest, LocalHarvest.org
Neighborhood Fruit, NeighborhoodFruit.com
Slow Food Nation, SlowFoodNation.org
Slow Food USA, SlowFoodUSA.org
Urban Homestead, UrbanHomestead.org
Veggie Trader, VeggieTrader.com
Yards to Gardens, y2g.org

THE SOY FIASCO

THE soy industry has done a really good job of promoting soy as a health food. A look into what soy may or may not do to human health might change your mind about soy.

For the best of health, you may want to avoid all soy products. While soy is found in many natural foods and is sold at "health foods" stores, it is found in an increasing amount of processed foods with claims that it is beneficial to health.

A person shouldn't automatically assume that soy is a health food. Soy contains the isoflavones daidzen and genestein, which are known as phytoestrogens because they can mimic estrogen in the body, binding with estrogen receptors on the cells – and may or may not play a role in breast and endometrial cancers. Studies are a bit confusing, with some concluding that the isoflavones in soy are antioxidants that protect tissues, are anti-inflammatory, and also help to reduce risk of cancer as they may block the receptors from binding with more potent natural estrogen, and also act to block the formation of estrogens forming in fatty tissue, which is one of the problems with estrogen production – especially in women who are overweight when they are past menopause. Epidemiological studies have concluded that women who consume more soy may be less likely to experience breast cancer. However, other dietary issues may have come into play in reducing cancer risk, such as the likelihood that those who include more soy in their diet may be apt to follow a more vegetarian or vegan diet, thus reducing their cancer risk by not eating meat, milk, eggs, and animal fats.

While men also are at risk for breast cancer, their concern with avoiding soy products usually revolves around the risk of the phytoestrogens, daidzen and genestein, playing roles in enlarged breasts (gynecomastia), decreased libido, weaker erections, ED, lower sperm counts, loss of body hair, and mood swings. For these hormonal reasons men may want to steer clear of soy products.

Studies concluding that men who consume soy may have lower rates of prostate cancer may also overlook the fact that men who consume soy are following more of a vegetarian or vegan diet, thus reducing their risk of prostate cancer because they aren't eating meat, milk, or eggs.

Men who think they need the protein in soy for their work out may want to consider what that soy protein powder really is doing to their body tissues and hormonal balance. Whey and casein protein powders are also not healthful, and increase the risk of cancer, arthritis, and other maladies. Men would be better off avoiding the soy, whey, or casein protein supplement powders and instead eating more leafy green vegetables and raw fruit for energy, protein, antioxidants, fiber, vitamins, minerals, amino acids, essential fatty acids, and other macro and micronutrients. Also, consider a raw vegan green powder supplement, such as Infinity Greens, Green Vibrance, or Healthforce VitaMineral Greens. And, consider a homemade granola containing activated pumpkin seeds, activated sunflower seeds, activated Brazil nuts, activated almonds, activated steel cut oats, diced dates, black currants, gojie berries, and freshly ground fenugreek, hemp, and flax seeds. Learn about and use the common weed purslane in your foods.

The biggest benefit of consuming that cheap soy protein powder crap is to the bank accounts of the stores and companies selling or marketing it. The estrodial production issues related to soy should be reasons enough for men to avoid it. The phytates in soy interfere with the absorption of minerals. The lectins and saponins in soy can interfere with the function of the digestive tract, and help to cause leaky gut syndrome, which can greatly increase the risk of experiencing arthritis and other autoimmune disorders. The protease inhibitors in soy interfere with the digestion of protein. If you are trying to improve your health, why would you consume soy protein powder?

Advice for men: don't drink soy milk, eat tofu, consume foods containing soy oil or other soy substances, or use soy protein powders.

Soy may negatively impact the thymus gland, which plays a role in the production of white blood cells, which are key to a healthy immune system. This is another reason why soy is not a good choice for baby formula. If a baby does not have access to breast milk, which should always be the first choice in baby food, a better choice than soy milk would be vegan milk with a base of hemp seeds. One glance at the ingredient list of common baby formula, including the amount of corn syrup and other junk substances, is reason enough to avoid using it. Infants fed soy-based formula may also have an increased risk of asthma and other health issues later in life.

In addition to those isoflavones, soy products often contain an abundance of enzyme inhibitors, phytates, and also substances called goitrogens that suppress both iodine uptake and thyroid function. Even soaking raw soybeans doesn't rid the beans of the substances; cooking them also doesn't rid them of the goitrogens. These are some of the reasons why many who are into natural foods seek to avoid soy. If they do consume soy, they go for the organic, non-GMO, fermented soy products, such as miso and tamari, and they use them sparingly. They also may choose to use non-soy versions, including garbanzo bean or brown rice miso in place of soy miso, or coconut aminos instead of tamari.

Nama shoyu is also a fermented soy product. If used, it should be unpasteurized and made from organic, non-GMO soy beans. I avoid nama shoyu. I don't like the way it tastes, and I don't like the way it makes me feel.

Be aware that many processed and packaged foods contain soy, including in the forms of hydrolyzed vegetable protein, lecithin, soy extract, soy protein, soy flour, soy cheese, tempeh, natto, nutrition bars, soy isolate, soy oil, and other forms of soy. Soy oil is usually hydrogenated, which is rich in transfats that promote cardiovascular disease that leads to heart attacks and strokes. Soy can be found in everything from processed fruit juices to potato chips to hamburgers – more reasons to avoid those products.

Soy products often contain a variety of other ingredients that are not good for health, including brown rice syrup sweetener in soy milk, and various colors, flavorings, scents, emulsifiers, and processed salts in soy meat products. Cooking soy at high temperatures creates a variety of heat-generated chemicals, including acrylamides and glycotoxins, which cause an immune response and can contribute to degenerative diseases.

Even foods that many consider to be healthy, such as the Naked Juice brand, which is owned by PepsiCo, has been found to contain soy, and not just any soy, but genetically modified soy, which likely carries residues of toxic farming chemicals, and may be damaging to gut flora and intestinal function. PepsiCo has famously donated to campaigns working against GMO labeling laws. Do the planet a favor and avoid products produced by PepsiCo.

Most soy today is of the GMO variety, and is grown using toxic farming chemicals, such as Monsanto's Glyphosate-based RoundUp Ready herbicide. If you still choose to consume soy, please use non-GMO soy that has been grown using organic methods.

The biggest benefit of soy is as a nitrogen fixer and fertilizer for soil in farming. As a human food, soy is not the best choice. Skip it.

READ LABELS

G ET used to reading labels, learning what is in your foods, and avoiding foods containing toxic ingredients.

Let's consider what is in a product many people use every day, coffee creamer. Following is a list of the ingredients of Coffee-Mate as listed on LabelWatch.com.

If you consider that sodium caseinate is derived from milk, you may ask why a milk product in a product labeled "dairy-free"?

Why are all of these synthetic chemicals in a product that is among the first things people put in their stomachs every morning?

You know that the corn syrup, cornstarch, soybean oil, and cottonseed oil are very likely from GMO crops sprayed with a variety of toxic farming chemicals.

What are those words, digylcerides and polysorbate 60?

If you know about the health issues related to consuming carrageenan, corn syrup, soybean oil, and hydrogenated oils, you would likely question why these substances are allowed in food products – at least without a mention of their toxicity and health warnings on labels, the way cigarette packaging is required to have.

"Coffee-mate, fat free liquid nondairy creamer. Ingredients: Water, corn syrup solids, partially hydrogenated soybean oil, and/or cottonseed oil, (adds a trivial amount of fat), less than 2 percent sugar, modified cornstarch, dipotassium phosphate, sodium caseinate (milk derivative), not a source of lactose, color added, artificial flavor, mono and digylcerides, polysorbate 60, sodium stearoyl lactylate, carrageenan, salt, betacarotene, color."

– LabelWatch.com

If you want to experience vibrant health, don't ingest foods containing synthetic chemicals, corn syrup, corn sweetener, corn oil, soy oil, casein, carrageenan, hydrogenated oils, partially hydrogenated oils, diglycerides, polysorbate, dairy, or extracts of dairy.

Distance yourself from processed foods.

If it doesn't grow from soil, don't eat it – especially if it is a chemical formulated in a lab.

EGGS, FISH OIL, AND HUMAN DISEASE

I hear people say that they are vegetarian, but they eat eggs and take fish oil supplements.

Could eating eggs and taking fish oil supplements be considered vegetarian - if you take into account what happens to obtain those eggs and that fish oil?

Are eggs or fish oil vegetation? Doesn't the word "vegetarian" indicate "vegetation"? Do eggs or fish grow on trees, bushes, or vines, or are they leafy greens or root vegetables? Do we pick them like apples, grapes, tomatoes, lettuce, or carrots? Are they formed from a pollinated flower? Are they leaves or twigs or branches? No. Chicken eggs come out of the reproductive organ of a chicken. Fish oil is extracted from the body tissues of killed fish.

Consider what it takes to obtain eggs.

Billions of male chicks are killed soon after hatching. Because they aren't needed on egg farms, male chicks are killed within hours or days of hatching, and their dead bodies are treated as trash.

Some egg farms simply toss the baby male chicks into grinder machines. Some hatcheries toss the baby male chicks into grinders by the thousands every day. Some toss them into plastic bags, by the hundreds, suffocating them. Some gas them. Billions of baby male chicks die this way every year. Simply because they are born as male. And that is only in the U.S.

The billions of female chicks are kept and raised for egg production. When their egg production slows, those incarcerated, egg-laying slaves are slaughtered, cut into pieces, and their muscle is sold as "chicken" – as in chicken sandwiches, chicken salad, chicken hot dogs, roasted chicken, chicken soup, chicken breast, chicken nuggets, fried chicken, buffalo wings, chicken gumbo, kung pao chicken, etc.

Would you like to live in a cage your entire life? How about if you had wings? Would you like living in those conditions, never able to spread your wings? Then, why do you think it is okay for the chicken industry to raise billions of chickens every year in cages, often stuffed two, three, or four chickens to cages that are stacked two, three, or four, or more levels on top of each other, with the chickens on the top level cages defecating onto the chickens in the lower cages? Would you like to be covered in poop your entire life, in a cage too small to for you to stretch, only to be used as some sort of egg-making mechanism, and then put in ankle brackets, upside down, and have your neck slit?

That is the egg industry. It is a filthy, smelly industry rife with abuse.

Like you, chickens breathe air, eat, see, mate, care for and play with their young, and feel pain.

If you went into one of the huge warehouses that we call "factory chicken farms," with thousands of birds crowded into stacks of cages, you would likely never forget the smell, the filth, and the sounds, and also the dreadfully stressed and weary glare in the eyes of those frustrated, sickly, caged birds.

If you saw how chickens are slaughtered on assembly-line-like contraptions that send the chickens hanging upside down from their feet past the neck slitter, the defeatherer, the scorching pots, and so forth, you would likely not forget that vision of animals being slaughtered and chopped into pieces. It's a bloody mess, and it also is difficult to avoid getting feces onto the meat – because dead bodies aren't very good at controlling their poopers.

It is no surprise that chicken meat is often found to harbor bacteria that can make people sick, can cause kidney and other organ failure, and can send some people to the grave. This is why it is advisable to practice cleanliness when preparing chicken meat in your kitchen, and to be sure to cook those dead animal bits at high enough temperatures to kill harmful bacteria. Unfortunately, for you, cooking that meat also creates free radicals, rancid fats, denatured amino acids, and heat-generated chemicals that also are not good for human health, trigger immune-system responses, and increase the risk of tissue damage, cancer, and other conditions and diseases.

Chickens and eggs aren't fruits, nor are they vegetables. Nor are they good for you to ingest.

When considering what eggs really are... you don't really want to think about what eggs are. Especially if you are putting eggs in your mouth.

One thing a chicken egg is for humans that eat them, as science is proving, is that they are a heart disease, stroke, and cancer promoter. Simply consider chicken eggs to be cancer and cardiovascular disease triggers. Cooked eggs are also rich in the free radicals that damage and age tissues, including the delicate macula area of the eyes, helping to degrade vision.

The lecithin in eggs breaks down into choline. What is found concentrated in human cancer cells? Choline. And it is more present in people consuming eggs. The choline situation is only one of the reasons eggs increase the risk of cancer.

Egg consumption raises the presence of TMAO (Trimethylamine N-oxide) in the blood. High levels of TMAO increase the risk of heart attacks, strokes, and cancers, such as cancers of the brain, breasts, uterus, ovaries, prostate, colon, kidneys, and bladder.

The concentrated protein and the cholesterol in eggs also increase the risk of cancer, heart disease, strokes, erectile dysfunction, and vision degradation. They can help trigger autoimmune disorders, including arthritis.

Did you notice that, men? Eggs increase the incidence of both erectile dysfunction and prostate cancer. You can easily find a number of studies making these conclusions.

Eggs contain no fiber. Milk and meat also do not contain fiber. A low-fiber diet is associated with increased risk of heart disease, strokes, cancer, macular (vision) degradation, erectile dysfunction, varicose veins, and other debilitating, degenerative and chronic health conditions.

What does contain the fiber that is so beneficial to health, and prevents disease? Fruits, vegetables, nuts, and seeds.

Those of you who are eating eggs for the protein may want to reconsider. You know what has more protein per calorie than an egg? Green leafy vegetables. For some reason, plant proteins do not carry the risks associated with protein from eggs, meat (including beef, pork, chicken, turkey, lamb, and fish), and dairy (all milk products, including butter, cheese, kefir, yogurt, cream, creamer, ice cream, whey, and casein). You may also want to try hemp seed powder, which is a good source of plant protein. Or, try a product like Billy Merritt's Infinity Greens (which you can find on the Internet, and in some natural foods stores).

The big, lean, strong muscles of a horse are made of the amino acids in the greens that horse ate. Same for gorillas, deer, antelope, giraffes, kangaroo, and other large and strong land mammals that are natural vegans.

People say that eggs are a good source of omega-3 fatty acids. Really? Maybe they would like to reconsider that claim, or... remain in denial.

Do you know why the egg industry started marketing eggs as "rich in omega-3s"? Well, they started feeding the chickens flax seeds and/or fishmeal. Clever.

To get omega-3s, you can skip eating the eggs and, instead, simply add freshly ground flax seeds to your foods, such as salads, smoothies, hummus, dips, fresh vegetable juices, dehydrated seed and veggie crackers, etc.

Feeding fish meal to chickens to get omega-3s is a rather obtuse, and energetically insufficient way of obtaining omega-3s. Taking fish from the sea to form into feed for farmed chickens that would otherwise never be eating sea creatures, is also a bit strange, and energy intensive.

The billions upon billions of fish that are being pulled from the oceans and turned into feed for farmed animals is helping to cause overfishing, and the regional or total extinction of species. Using so many sea creatures to make feed for farmed animals is depleting the oceans of food for other creatures that rely on those fish, including seals, turtles (all sea turtles are endangered), dolphin, predator fish, and marine birds.

Why are we feeding an increasing number of sea creatures to pigs, cows, turkeys, chickens, and other animals that would never naturally ingest sea creatures? Why are we using so much fuel and other resources to send ships into the oceans to kill so many creatures, and turn them into feed, and transport that feed into the continents, where it is fed to farmed animals?

We certainly do not need to be feeding fish meal to chickens so that we can then claim that the eggs those chickens produce are "rich in omega oils."

Fish get the omega-3s from the greens they eat, as in seaweeds and algaes. That is how omega-3s get into fish.

You can skip eating the fish, and simply add some seaweeds (such as dulse and kelp) and algaes (such as chlorella, spirulina, and blue-green algae) to your foods. If you aren't into seaweeds or algaes, you can also get omega-3s from fresh raw greens (including raw kale, chard, spinach, broccoli greens, collards, cabbage, lettuces, oregano, parsley, basil, cilantro, fennel greens, mustard greens, beet greens, dandelion greens, etc.), raw fruit, raw sprouts, and raw germinated seeds (such as chia and buckwheat). You can also obtain omega-3s from flax seeds and hemp seeds. And from raw walnuts. And by adding the common weed, purslane, to your foods, here and there, such as by tossing some purslane into a salad, or blending into a fruit smoothie.

Consuming fish oil isn't a good way of obtaining omega-3s. What that oil also contains is the industrial pollutants, heavy metals, and other toxins the fish was exposed to in the water it swam in, and in the substances it ingested.

Unfortunately, even fish caught in the Arctic and Antarctica are found to contain industrial pollutants, such as fire retardants, heavy metals, PCBs, and other toxins. These pollutants are harming seals, whales, bears, foxes, marine birds, and other animals that are eating fish. An increasing number of these wild animals are found to have cancer, to have difficulty carrying to term, to have babies with deformities, and to be underweight.

You may hear a fish oil supplement company claim that their fish oil is obtained from fish swimming in pristine waters. Really? If the fish of the Arctic and Antarctic are found to contain a variety of pollutants, where on the planet do you think those companies are obtaining these fish, especially if the seas most distant from cities are found to contain fish with measurable residues of heavy metals, industrial pollutants, fire retardants, PCBs, and other toxins? The marketing claims of the fish oil supplement companies may sound all nice and pretty, but they are a fantasy and nothing but a sales pitch. Even fish captured off the most remote islands of the planet are found to contain industrial toxins.

Fish oil supplements also increase the risk of bleeding, such as from cuts, and also bleeding in the brain. For some interesting information, look up "Fish oil supplements and brain hemorrhage." Hemorrhage is one of the very real risk factors of taking fish oil supplements.

A friend of mine in his 30s had a cerebral hemorrhage that doctors attributed to his use of fish oil supplements. His doctors looked up studies concluding this and showed the studies to my friend. They advised him to refrain from using fish oil supplements, and to choose plant-based omega-3s.

My friend was in the hospital for three months. He was left with a $140,000.oo (one hundred and forty thousand dollar) hospital bill, in addition to the cost of a variety of pharmaceuticals. He spent months going through physical therapy to regain his muscle coordination and strength. The experience devastated his life.

The human nutritional requirement for animal protein is absolute zero. The human nutritional requirement for fish oil supplements is absolute zero. The human nutritional requirement for eggs is absolute zero. The human nutritional requirement for chicken is absolute zero. The human nutritional requirement for fish is absolute zero.

What contains the nutrients your body needs to thrive?

Fruits, vegetables, nuts, and seeds contain the vitamins, minerals, essential fatty acids, amino acids, antioxidants, fiber, carbohydrates, and other nutrients your body needs to thrive.

You don't need to support fishing fleets that deplete the oceans of wildlife, and you don't need to support the egg and poultry industries. What would be beneficial is to grow some of your own foods using organic growing methods, as fresh fruits and vegetables are the most healthful of all foods.

PLANT-BASED FOODS AND HEALTH: NATURE PROVIDES OUR FOOD

INADEQUATE nutrition and the consumption of junk food contribute to everything from skin problems to heart disease, and from depression to birth defects. Eating whole foods, such as unprocessed fruits and vegetables and whole grains, provides the body with important nutrients such as vitamins, minerals, fiber, amino acids, essential fatty acids, and enzymes; and phytochemicals, including isoflavonoids and lignans.

Tremendous health benefits can be gained by consuming a diet rich in substances originating in raw, edible plants – and especially so if the diet is free of the health-damaging substances contained in meat, milk, and eggs. These beneficial plant substances are natural chemicals called antioxidants. These chemicals only exist in animals in trace amounts, and only because the animal ate plants containing the antioxidants. It is antioxidants that shield us from free radicals that naturally occur in our bodies, and also that are introduced to our systems through low quality foods, including meat, dairy, and eggs, and also by way of substance abuse, such as by smoking and drinking alcohol. Free radicals damage body tissues, including the muscles, cardiovascular system, skin, and the mechanisms within the eyes. This is one reason why antioxidants called carotenoids, which are found in carrots and other vegetables and fruits, are said to help the eyes. Free radicals also play a role in cancer. Antioxidants are so centric to good nutrition that they are a basic key to maintaining vibrant health and a strong immune system. Without a diet rich in raw plant matter, you are lacking in the spectrum of beneficial antioxidants that can only be obtained through the consumption of plants.

Someone may say that there are some antioxidants in meat. They are not incorrect in saying this. But it is like comparing a raindrop to a lake, with a piece of meat being the raindrop, and an apple or other raw fruit or vegetable being a lake of beneficial nutrients. Any antioxidants in the meat got there only by way of the animal eating plants. Animals, including humans, do not conduct photosynthesis, which is the process that takes place in plant cells when they absorb sun energy and store it, forming the colors in the plants. Therefore, antioxidants, which are in the natural colors of plants, are vastly more available in edible, raw plant substances, and much less present in meat, dairy, and eggs. Consuming animal protein to try to access antioxidants is less effective than licking the juice from a knife that just cut through a piece of fruit, instead of simply eating the fruit itself.

By consuming animal protein, you are also consuming free radicals, which exist and form in meat, milk, and eggs. So, even if you are consuming some trace amounts of certain antioxidants in the animal protein, you are countering it by also consuming the damaging free radicals in that animal flesh, dairy, or eggs. This scenario does not equal good nutrition – especially considering that meat, dairy, and eggs also contain saturated fat, cholesterol, and a variety of other substances that work against health.

Studies are constantly revealing how certain fruits and vegetables (broccoli, peppers, onions, garlic, carrots, cranberries, apples, pomegranates, cucumbers, tomatoes, beets, squash, ginger, beans, broccoli, sprouts, spinach, collards, cauliflower, chard, kale, dandelion, cilantro, berries, etc.) not only provide needed nutrients that are beneficial to health, but also that they contain and provide properties that prevent certain serious ailments, such as diabetes, cancer, Alzheimer's, MS, and heart disease; limit intestinal exposure to carcinogens; and help the body to contain, transport, and eliminate toxins.

> "A number of studies have shown that cancer risk is lower and immune competence is higher in individuals who consume a vegetarian diet. Epidemiological studies almost unanimously report a strong correlation between a diet high in fruits and vegetables and low cancer risk."
> – John Boik, in his book *Cancer & Natural Medicine: A Textbook of Basic Research and Clinical Research*

Eat a vegetarian diet and you will be doing what many world-class athletes are doing. For instance, Dave Scott, who has won the Hawaiian Ironman contest six times and is considered to be among the best athletes who ever lived, is a complete vegetarian.

In July 2011, Michael Arnstein, a low-fat raw vegan who has the site TheFruitarian.com, won the Vermont 100 Ultra Marathon. For the past two years, he and his wife, Victoria, have thrown the Woodstock Fruit Festival, which is a week of seminars, sports, and good times in upstate New York. In 2012, Michael and Victoria both ran the Vermont 100, days after Michael ran the Badwater race in California.

Ultramarathon champion Scott Jurek won the Western States race seven straight times. In 2005 Jurek also won the grueling 135-mile Badwater race, which begins at the lowest elevation in the Western Hemisphere, in Death Valley, California, and ends 8,300 feet up a mountain, and he did it faster than anyone in the history of the race. Then he won it again in 2006. He did this all while following a vegan diet.

On October 16, 2011, Fauja Singh finished the Scotiabank Toronto Waterfront Marathon in about eight hours. You may think that eight hours is a slow time for completing a marathon. Well, consider that at the time of the race, he was 100 years old! He credited a vegetarian diet as being key to his longevity, stamina, and ability.

Vegan athletes include Australian Division One biker and marathon runner, Harley "Durianrider" Johnstone of 30BananasADay.com; triathlete Brendan Brazier of

MyVega.com; Ironwoman Ruth Heidrich; tennis pro Martina Navratilova; heavyweight boxing champ Peter Hussig; karate champ Ridgely Abele; Heisman trophy winner Desmond Howard; running back, Montell Owens; Olympic wrestler Chris Campbell; Mr. Universe Bill Pearl; gymnast Dan Millman; bodybuilders Evan Connelly Novacek and Kristopher Flannery; marathon champ Jane Wetzel; Olympic skater Surya Bonaly; boxer Keith Holmes; mixed martial arts champ Mac Danzig; and many more. In 2011, boxer Mike Tyson said he had been following a vegan diet for two years, and that it has helped him to heal on many levels. In 2012, as he worked to correct his ways, Lance Armstrong spoke of the benefits of increased energy he has experienced by switching to a lower fat, organic, mostly vegan diet. Armstrong had been training with Rip Esselstyn, an athlete and the author of *The Engine 2 Diet*, which advocates a 100 percent vegan, low-fat diet.

"Even when you're training really hard, it's normal that you would have certain things for lunch or certain things for breakfast, and then have this dip, or almost like a food coma. I don't experience that anymore. My energy level has never been this consistent, and not just consistent, but high. I'm a big napper – I couldn't even take a nap these days if I wanted to.

The other thing – I expected to get rid of that dip, but I didn't expect the mental side of it, and the sharpness and the focus that I've noticed. And I was the biggest nonbeliever, I was like 'whatever, man,' and I'm in. I'm not doing dinners yet, but breakfast and lunch, I'm in."

– Lance Armstrong, speaking of following a largely low-fat vegan diet while training for a marathon, March 2012

"I have been a vegan for almost two years now and the benefits have been tremendous. I have more stamina and it helps keep me in a positive state of mind. I didn't realize how weighed down I was when I ate meat. I never

really felt 100 percent until I freed it from my diet. Now, I can't imagine going back to meat. I feel incredible."
– Mike Tyson, World heavyweight boxing champion; quotation 2011

"Today you have processed meats and a lot of animals suffering unnecessarily for it. Now, some people just blow that off and don't have a conscience about it, or they just don't care. They wouldn't eat their dog, but they feel that way about other animals. But for me, I decided to stop eating meat. I didn't want to contribute to all of that. I'm not trying to change the world, or wear that on my sleeve, or make a political statement, because that just turns people away. I only have control over one person, and that's myself. And I feel good about it."
– Mac Danzig, vegan mixed martial arts champ

"I've found that a person does not need protein from meat to be a successful athlete. In fact, my best year of track competition was the first year I ate a vegan diet."
– Carl Lewis, nine-time Olympic gold medal winner

Although it is reasonable to assume that there have always been people who have followed a diet consisting of only plant substances, the modern vegan diet is often attributed to the teachings of Donald Watson, who died at age 95 in Cumbria on November 16, 2005. He became a vegetarian after seeing his Uncle George involved in the slaughter of a pig. Hearing the pig's screams haunted him. "I decided that farms – and uncles – had to be reassessed: The idyllic scene was nothing more than death row, where every creature's days were numbered."

Eventually, Watson eliminated dairy from his diet. When his elder brother and a sister also became vegetarians, his mother, who was not a vegetarian, made the comment that she felt like a hen who had hatched a clutch of duck eggs.

"We may be sure that should anything so much as a pimple ever appear to mar the beauty of our physical form, it will be entirely due in the eyes of the world to our

own silly fault for not eating 'proper food.' Against such a pimple the great plagues of diseases now ravaging nearly all members of civilized society (who eat 'proper food') will pass unnoticed."
    – Donald Watson, founder of "veganism,"
    acknowledging the critical microscope vegans were
    put under by those who consume the so-called
    "proper foods" of milk, eggs, and meat

As an adult, Watson became a woodworking instructor. In 1939 he registered as a conscientious objector and refused to go to war. At the end of the war he formed a group of "nondairy vegetarians." The group advocated the health benefits of such a diet, and taught that animal agriculture was likely to spread diseases, such as the tuberculosis that was identified in Britain's dairy cows. He concocted the term "vegan" by taking the beginning and end of the word "vegetarian." Terms that he and his group considered included "beaumangeur," "benevor," "dairyban," "sanivore," and "vitan." The first edition of The Vegan Society's *Vegan News* was published in 1944 and consisted of 12 typed pages bound using staples.

When you consume a diet that consists of what nature provides, and the closer it is to its natural state, the nearer your body will be to its natural state.

    "My doctor told me to stop having intimate dinners
    for four. Unless there are three other people present."
    – Orson Welles

The natural state of the body is to be healthy and free from toxins and disease. The keys to health are healthful thought pattern, exercise regimen, diet, relationships, and atmosphere. You can't follow a more healthful diet than one consisting purely of a variety of quality organically grown vegetables, fruits, herbs, nuts, seeds, and water vegetables – especially if some are homegrown.

To experience the abundance that nature can provide for you, abundantly take advantage of what nature provides. What nature provides is a pathway to pristine health paved with nutritious foods consisting of plant substances. These are the substances that our bodies are genetically designed to eat. Anything else, such as processed foods, and those that contain artificial coloring, flavoring, textures, scents, preservatives, and so forth are not natural and should not be put into the body.

Don't try to get too complicated in regard to your food choices. Refuse to buy into the false information about various food companies trying to sell products that are filled with chemicals and chemically grown foods. Simply choose what is presented to us in nature. Fruits, vegetables, nuts, and seeds are in tune with nature, and this is especially true if they are organically grown, and not genetically altered.

Eating what is in tune with nature tunes us into nature and our natural state of being. That is the truth about food.

> "When I buy cookies I eat just four and throw the rest away. But first I spray them with Raid so I won't dig them out of the garbage later. Be careful, though, because Raid really doesn't taste that bad."
>
> – Janette Barber, writer and stand-up comic

It is simple. If you eat a healthful diet, you will experience better health than if you eat a diet of junk. This concept isn't part of the pop commercial diets promoted in books and through fad diet plans, which are based on ignorance, laziness, and greed. That is because people can't make money by simply telling you to eat organic fruits and vegetables – other than organic produce farmers, who deserve to be paid for their work. The most expensive diet plans out there consist of manufactured foods that have been deadened through cooking and processing. They lead to diseases of affluence, such as obesity, heart disease, Type 2 diabetes, Alzheimer's, and colorectal cancer.

Many diet book authors are selling manufactured and processed food products and supplements that go with their "diet plan." But this book is not selling you any food products, pills, potions, or supplements. I am simply telling you to eat organically grown plant substances. I'm also suggesting that you grow as much of your own food as reasonable, and use organic growing methods to do so. It is best not to be completely reliant on stores and restaurants for your most basic needs, such as food. (Access: KitchenGardeners.org, VegetableGardener.com, UrbanHomestead.org, FoodNotLawns.com, and Yards to Gardens: Y2G.org. See the book: *The Edible Front Yard: The Mow-Less, Grow-More Plan for a Beautiful, Bountiful Garden*, by Ivette Soler.)

While acknowledging that people may not care to limit themselves to just a few types of fruits for their nourishment, it is still interesting to consider that just a few healthy fruit trees can supply a person with a lot more food than he or she could possibly eat in a lifetime. I have friends whose homes are surrounded by fruit trees producing so much fruit that they can't give away the fruit fast enough. They get as much as they need and abundantly more. And they aren't considered farmers.

If you want to have a lively, vibrant body, then you should be eating living, vibrant foods. The liveliest foods you can give to your body are those found in nature: vibrantly alive plant substances that have not been degraded by high temperatures, chemicals, or genetic engineering.

If you are confused by all the diet and health information you have heard and read about in pop culture, there is a reason you are confused, because nature is not confusing. Only the information put out by man is confusing. Forget about what advertising and fad diet plans have told you about nutrition. When choosing food, simply stick to nature. What nature provides for you will not do you wrong.

> "If you love your children, don't let them eat animals. You wouldn't let your children have cigarettes, yet meat-based diets cause more deaths from cancer each year than smoking."
> – EvolveCampaigns.org.uk

Learn to eat naturally, and rely on foods that are as close to their natural state as possible. When you do so, your body will begin to conform to its natural state.

Stop allowing yourself to be caught up in all of the complex diets promoted by the various pop culture diet gurus and multinational food companies that want you to buy and eat their products so that they can make more money. Ignore food advertising. Skip over all of the processed foods you face at the supermarket. Go straight to the produce section. Request that your local market sell more organic produce. Shop at farmers' markets. Join or start a CSA, or an organic food co-op. (Consider the Rawfully Organic Food Co-op in Houston that was started by Kristina Carillo-Bucaram. Access: RawFullyOrganic.com.)

Teach children how to grow food gardens, to forage wild edibles, and to prepare foods from scratch in alignment with a plant-based diet.

HUMANS ARE HERBIVORES, NOT CARNIVORES OR OMNIVORES

THE teeth and mouths of humans are very different from the teeth and mouths of carnivores, such as animals in the cat, dog, and bear families. Carnivores have sharp teeth and wide mouths framed by snouts and can bite, lock, and tear at meat. Some people say the omnivore shape of human teeth suggests that humans are meant for a diet of both plant and meat content. Other people say that because human teeth are short and smooth, the human jaw swivels in a grinding motion, and the mouths are small and relatively weak, humans therefore are more structured for eating plants. (Animals that eat plants are known as herbivores.)

> "You can't tear flesh by hand, you can't tear hide by hand. Our anterior teeth are not suited for tearing flesh or hide. We don't have large canine teeth, and we wouldn't have been able to deal with food sources that required those large canines."
> – Dr. Richard Leakey

Carnivores eat meat when it is raw. Humans are not natural meat eaters. When humans do eat meat they do so only after it has been tenderized or ground, then softened even more by cooking with high temperatures – and then, at last, sliced – and often saturated with flavoring, like catsup, mustard, hot sauce, or herbs. Humans don't like the taste of raw meat, and they hide the flavor – including by cooking it.

Even after preparing, cooking, and cutting meat, humans often have a hard time chewing and swallowing the stuff – sometimes losing teeth and gagging to death during the process (the animals' revenge?).

93

The human mouth structures are only part of the picture. Those who say humans are meant to eat a plant-based diet may have their beliefs verified by taking the human digestive tract into consideration.

Human bowels are very different from the smooth and relatively straight bowels of meat-eating animals. The human digestive tract is more than 10-times body length. Carnivores have a digestive tract that may be as long as their body. The puckered, long, and curved structures of the human digestive tract indicate that humans are more attuned to eating a fiber-rich plant-based diet. The stomach acids of the human are also much weaker than those of carnivores, and are more in balance with the stomach acid levels of herbivores.

Carnivore saliva is acidic. Carnivore saliva does not contain ptyalin. Human saliva is alkaline and human salivary glands produce ptyalin. Ptyalin breaks the hydrolysis of dextrin and starch, turning the long-chain sugars into smaller soluble sugar fragments. This is key to a creature meant to consume a diet based on starch – not meat or eggs.

Humans need fiber to help digest food. Meat, dairy, and eggs do not contain fiber. Humans who do not eat enough fiber have higher rates of serious diseases, including cardiovascular disease, colorectal cancer, breast cancer, diabetes, and kidney disease, and also are more likely to have strokes and heart attacks. A vegan diet rich in raw fruits and vegetables easily contains an abundance of fiber.

The carnivore liver produces uricase (uricase oxidase), which metabolizes the uric acid that is a byproduct of the breakdown of purines in meats. Organ meats are rich in purines, so are anchovies, herring, mackerel, mussels, sardines, and scallops. Carnivores love organ meats. Other meats, including beef, pork, game meats (deer, etc.), shellfish, fish, and poultry all contain purines. So does meat gravy. Human don't produce uricase. When uric acid builds up in humans, they can end up with an abundance of urate crystals in their system, and that results in or contributes to situations including varicose veins, cardiovascular disease, bursitis, arthritis, gout (a type of arthritis), diabetes, kidney stones, and kidney failure.

While some purines can be found in plant sources like asparagus, cauliflower, green peas, lentils, oats, and spinach, the alkaline diet that is a low-fat vegan diet rich in raw fruits and vegetables protects against the health problems associated with a diet rich in meats. Because of accompanying components in plants, fruits and vegetable purines are excreted more easily than are purines from meat sources. Vegans typically have a low level of uric acid in the bloodstream.

Unlike carnivores, humans do not have claws that can tear into another animal to kill it and rip it open. Humans have prehensile hands, with soft fingers topped by fingernails perfect for peeling fruit.

Carnivores can survive perfectly on raw meat and water. If a human consumed nothing but meat and water, they would experience a variety of health problems, and likely would not live very long.

> "A recent study by Smith found that high-fat, high-protein, low-carbohydrate (HPLC) diets (which are usually high in red meat, such as the Atkins and Paleolithic diets) may accelerate atherosclerosis through mechanisms that are unrelated to the classic cardiovascular risk factors. Mice that were fed an HPLC diet had almost twice the level of arterial plaque as mice that were fed a Western diet even though the classic risk factors were not significantly different between groups. The mice that were fed the HPLC diet had markedly fewer circulating endothelial progenitor cells and higher levels of nonesterified fatty acids (promoting inflammation) than mice that were fed the Western diet."
>
> – Dr. Dean Ornish, Holy Cow! What's Good For You Is Good For Our Planet: Comment on "Red Meat Consumption and Mortality," *Archives of Internal Medicine*, March 12, 2012. Ornish is the founder of the Preventative Medicine Research Institute, PMRI.org

Humans are not carnivores or omnivores. Humans are herbivores and they flourish in health on a low-fat vegan diet rich in raw fruits and vegetables. The human nutritional requirement for animal protein is absolute zero.

"A vegetarian diet has been advocated by everyone from philosophers such as Plato and Nietzsche, to political leaders such as Benjamin Franklin and Gandhi, to modern pop icons such as Paul McCartney and Bob Marley. Science is also on the side of vegetarianism. A multitude of studies have proven the health benefits of a vegetarian diet to be remarkable."
    – VegInfo.org/Health

"Man's structure, internal and external compared with that of other animals, shows that fruit and succulent vegetables are his natural food."
    – Carolus Linnaeus

"I became a vegetarian after realizing that animals feel afraid, cold, hungry, and unhappy like we do."
    – Cesar Chavez

"If we so easily take the lives of animals, who are only a few evolutionary steps from us, what is to prevent us from doing the same to humans?"
    – Peter Singer

"All available scientific evidence indicates that humans are frugivorous apes. Regardless of how large and arrogant our cultural egos are, and regardless of unsupportable religious dogma created by ignorant people who knew absolutely nothing of biochemistry, comparative anatomy, genetics, or science thousands of years ago, our physiology is that of a frugivorous ape."
    – Laurie Forti

PLANT-BASED DIET IS THE WAY TO HEALTH

"I regard animals as persons of another species. And I don't eat their flesh for the same reasons that I don't eat the flesh of people. I know that nonhuman animals value their lives and their freedom and their families. And I know that life is as much an adventure and a joy for them as it can be for us. I wish to honor their interests as well as my own and help create a more peaceful place where we can all live."

– Don Robertson

"It is the hidden horror that the egg industry does not want you to see. In egg production male chicks are surplus to requirements, which means that they are sorted from the females in vast warehouses and then killed by the thousand at just a day or two old. Identical to the chicks you see on Easter greeting cards, these uncomprehending young birds are either sent on a conveyor belt to be gassed or thrown alive into electric mincers. The same system is used to sort those which move to barn, free range, or even most organic egg farms. It is an unimaginable waste of life – and all just to bring an egg to your morning table."

– Justin Kerswell

97

"It seems rather bizarre to me, and somewhat Jekyll and Hyde, to be sitting at your table devouring a creature while at the same time lovingly stroking another as your

pet. But then again, when one's raised that way, I guess the irony (some would say hypocrisy) isn't so easily seen."
– Lance Landall

"When a vegan is talking to a meat-eater about these issues, he or she is not 'preaching,' 'trying to convert,' or any such thing. We're not telling you what to eat. We're telling you what you're eating. Since animals can't speak a language humans can understand (though I think the screams and terrified moans that fill slaughterhouses should be pretty much universal – all living beings want to live), it's up to us to tell their stories and inform people of the suffering that goes on conveniently out of the public eye. If as a meat eater, being exposed to this reality bothers you, it is not the fault of the vegan."
– Ari Solomon

PUTTING meat, dairy, and eggs out of your life clears your spirit and detoxifies your body from the heinously bad energy associated with the entrapment, confinement, suffering, and killing of farm animals; from the horrors of the slaughterhouse; and from the sickly energy of the caged farm animals that are fed lousy, unnatural diets, are treated with drugs, and are sprayed with chemicals. A plant-based diet releases you from the bad energy of misusing Earth's resources in the way it is done by the mass breeding and killing of animals. And it releases you from the support and/or involvement of the packaging, marketing, cooking, and consumption of meat from billions of farmed animals (mammals, birds, and farmed fish).

"Once we recognize how poor the reasons are for killing 'food animals,' we glimpse the deeper explanation of why so few people actually visit slaughterhouses – and why so many want to remain blissfully ignorant of what transpires there. Every thoughtful person understands the truth of Emerson's observations: 'You have just dined, and however scrupulously the slaughterhouse is concealed in the graceful distance of miles, there is complicity.' That sense of our own complicity is what, deep down, we hope to shield from ourselves by refusing to look the death of animals in the eye. Before any rational reflection begins we understand that, if we looked, we would see the animals' blood on our hands. We would be aghast at ourselves for what we have done. And for what we are doing. So we look, not inside but aside, in search of every excuse not to face our involvement in the needless massacre (for that is what it is) of millions upon millions of animals, day in and day out. Opaque walls make good neighbors."

    – Tom Regan

When you work your life in tune with the energy of nature and follow a plant-based, natural diet, you are tuned into your natural instinct. Your body and brain will function better. You will be able to think more clearly. You will be healthier and have more energy. You will experience a synchronicity with your thoughts, actions, feelings, goals, and talents. A healthier you will manifest from inside as you shed the physical and spiritual residues you carried from living and eating unhealthfully.

When you follow a diet consisting of only or mostly raw plant substances, you are eating what is grown in nature and what will be synchronized with the patterns of the microscopic structures of your body tissues. As you sustain a diet consisting of totally or almost completely raw plants you will be infusing your system with the wavelengths of light and life that infuse all life forms.

The longer you maintain a diet of healthful foods rich in raw fruits and vegetables, the sooner you will be able to detect the changes in your body when you don't eat the best quality of foods. When you are eating a healthful, plant-based diet rich in raw fruits and vegetables, your body can better communicate what is good and healthful and what is not. As you become attuned to how your body feels after you consume certain foods, you will naturally want to stick with the foods that make you feel good. Your body will acclimate to eating and desiring that which is healthy.

Following a sunfood diet increases your vibrancy. By eliminating the deadness of cooked food from your diet, you will be subsisting on the unadulterated nutrients of plant matter radiant with the vibrational patterns of Sun and Nature. You will experience a new health destination and your life will align in accordance with it.

On a vegan diet rich in raw fruits and raw vegetables your life becomes alive.

Once you get a taste of how good your life can become, you will instinctively want to increase the good. Your perceptions of what you are capable of accomplishing and your abilities to do so awaken and become clear to you.

By working with the natural resources within you that give you the desire to succeed and experience happiness, and guiding yourself with those desires through goal setting and intentional daily actions, your life can improve in ways you previously may have thought were not possible.

Realize that life is full of possibilities for those who believe in their divinity, and who seek and believe and work toward making things happen through intentional actions using intellect, goal setting, talents, skill, and craft.

Be daring, brave, and wise. Bring yourself out of the box you have kept yourself in. Break down the walls of dullness. Decide now to enliven your energy. Stop eating dead foods. Allow yourself to experience the benefits of the sunfood diet rich in raw fruits and vegetables that infuse health. It will ignite your life and propel you into experiencing amazing things.

For more about radically transforming your life, read my book *Igniting Your Life: Pathways to the Zenith of Health and Success.*

"One day the absurdity of the almost universal human belief in the slavery of other animals will be

palpable. We shall then have discovered our souls and become worthier of sharing this planet with them."
  – Martin Luther King, Jr.

"Animals are not humans with reduced capacities. They have their own capacities, their own spectrum of aptitudes and behaviors."
  – Jean Kazaz

"I enjoy the health benefits of a vegan life and the knowledge that I am drastically lowering my carbon footprint, of course, it's the ethical principle of not subsidizing cruelty to animals that means the most to me."
  – Dan Piraro

"When animals express their feelings they pour out like water from a spout. Animals' emotions are raw, unfiltered, and uncontrolled. Their joy is the purest and most contagious of joys and their grief the deepest and most devastating. Their passions bring us to our knees in delight and sorrow."
  – Mark Bekoff

A PLEA FOR
NATURAL FOODS SYSTEMS

THERE are an increasing number of farms along the Central California coast having a tough time of it, and more are being offered money by land developers aiming to build housing tracts, corporate campuses, resorts, golf courses, shopping centers, and car lots.

On every continent of the planet, some of the best land for growing food year-round is being paved and covered with structures and roads. It is one of the most absurd activities humans have ever engaged in.

In the 1970s, much of Southern California's Orange County, Ventura County, and the Valencia region were farmland. A lot of that has since been covered with car lots, parking lots, housing tracts, corporate campuses, chain stores, fast food restaurants, mini-malls, malls, medical centers, golf courses, roads, and highways. It is similar to what happened to the San Fernando Valley and San Gabriel Valley in the 1950s and 1960s, and to the Los Angeles basin in the 1930s and 1940s.

The urban sprawl situation isn't only happening in California, but is happening wherever farms exist on land that has the potential of being "developed" into resorts, corporate campuses, malls, housing tracts, and other residential, commercial, recreational, and government developments, and the roads, utilities, and other infrastructures to support them.

American family farms are in a predicament of selling out, closing shop, or otherwise disappearing for a number of reasons. In 2010, the average age of a U.S. farmer was 57. One-fourth of them were over age 65. The younger ones, or the generation that would have taken over the farm, smell the money from the land developers. Some farmers, and those that inherit the farms, also turn into commercial and residential developers, turning their land into urban sprawl. Also, the natural gas industry keeps offering money to financially stressed farmers to allow fracking beneath their land, which leaves behind a stew of toxic chemicals that poison the land, water, air, wildlife, and people.

Massive industrial monocropping has been taking over farmland for decades, and more of it is happening in other countries. Companies like Monsanto, Cargill, ADM, Bunge, and Bayer CropScience are perpetuating a system of industrial food – toxic from all of the chemicals and the genetically engineered crops.

If you don't understand what Monsanto, DuPont, Novartis, Zeneca, BASF, Aventis, DOW Chemical, Bayer CropScience, ADM, Cargill, Bunge, and other corporations that are the monsters of the industrialized foods industries are doing to the food plants and seeds of Earth, and what they are doing to family farmers, water systems, soil organisms, and wildlife all over the planet, please learn. What they are doing is impacting you, no matter what part of the planet you live on.

Industrial monocropping is NOT a good thing. Not only because of the chemicals being used to do it, and not only because of the genetically engineered crops planted there, but also because of what it does to the soil, water, air, and wildlife. It also impacts and alters the soil organisms, which assist plants in absorbing nutrients. It can also alter the beneficial bacteria in your intestinal tract, which is the "intestinal flora" you need to help digest foods, absorb nutrients, produce enzymes, and metabolize beneficial substances.

Organic polycropping (chemical-free organic farming of a variety of rotated crops with non-GMO foods) is vastly more healthful for the soil, water, air, wildlife, and people – and for soil organisms and intestinal flora. Organic polycropping is also better for the plants, and their genetic makeup. Polycropping is what people did before industrial agriculture. Industrial agriculture is taking over family farms, obliterating large tracts of land, including forests and wetlands, and ridding the land of animals who interfere with growing massive monocropped fields.

These are some of the reasons why it is good to support local organic farmers (including by volunteering on them, by shopping at farmers' markets, and by avoiding corporate supermarkets), and why it is good to set up organic food co-ops, such as what Kristina Carrillo-Bucaram has done with The Rawfully Organic Food Co-op in Texas (Access: RawfullyOrganic.com). It is also good to learn how to make real food from scratch, such as what is taught at Cherie Soria's Living Light Culinary Institute in California (Access: RawFoodChef.com), and what is being done in raw vegan cafes in many countries (see my book *Sunfood Traveler: Global Guide to Raw Food Culture*).

What is happening to the food systems of the world is also why it is good to polycrop whatever bit of land you can. Turn your lawn into a food oasis. Join in with neighbors to plant a variety of culinary plants. Add a greenhouse to your property to extend your growing season. If you have a flat roof, turn that into a food garden. Rent a community garden. Turn local wildlands into food forests and nurture wild edible plants.

Find a local chapter of Food Not Lawns near you, or start a chapter. (Access: FoodNotLawns.com/local-chapters.html).

Bioneers.org
CRFG.org
EatTheWeeds.org
FallenFruit.org
FoodIsPower.org
TheFutureOfFood.com
KitchenGardeners.org
LocalHarvest.org
OccupyMonsanto360.org
OrganicConsumers.org
OrganicGardening.com
PANNA.org
SavingOurSeed.org

SayNoToGMOs.org
SeedSavers.net
SeedSavers.org
SynergySeeds.com
Tilth.org
UnderwoodGardens.com
UnitedPlantSavers.org
UrbanOrganicGardener.com
VandanaShiva.org
VegetarianUSA.com
VictorySeeds.com
WWOOF.org
y2g.org

(Many more organizations and helpful sites are listed in *Sunfood Traveler.*)

Many U.S. farmers went into debt to the federal government because the Farm Home Administration counseled farmers to take out loans in the 1970s when the value of the farms was inflating faster than the interest rates. Then the government raised interest rates on the farmers and foreclosed on family farms at record levels. That is truly a sad and sickening part of U.S. history.

Under the massive takeover of farms by multinational corporations, family farmers are struggling to maintain and update equipment to pay for water, to keep up with packing fees, to pay for labor and transportation, and to compete with pricing. This is a driving force in the formation of rural groups that have found good reason to mistrust the government – which has a history of not providing the truth to its citizens, but does have a history of protecting corporate interests.

> "Family farms are an important part of the American tradition of self-sufficiency, forming the bedrock for communities across the U.S.
>
> Since 1935, the U.S. has lost 4.7 million farms. Fewer than one million Americans now claim farming as a primary occupation.
>
> Farmers in 2002 earned their lowest real net cash income since 1940. Meanwhile, corporate agribusiness profits have nearly doubled (increased 98 percent) since 1990.
>
> Large corporations increasingly dominate U.S. food production.
>
> … Encourage your local grocery store and area restaurants to purchase more of their products from local farmers."
>
> – FoodRoutes.Org, 2006

In addition to losing their farms to the corporate farming industry takeover, farmers have been selling out to housing developers who offer more money for the farmland than the farm can make in several years of operating at a tight budget.

So the housing tracts get built on the farmland and the streets are given pleasant country names like Wildflower Lane, Cherry Orchard Court, and Apple Blossom Road.

All of this gives reason why family farmers in the U.S. should be permitted to freely grow industrial hemp, which is NOT a drug plant, but is a plant that is grown for materials to make, among other things, food, clothing, paper, fuel, paint, ink, insulation, plywood (fiberboard that is stronger, more resilient to rot and infestation, and more environmentally safe than plywood made from trees), resin, fiberglass, skin and hair products, flooring, building blocks (stronger, lighter, and more environmentally safe to produce than building blocks made from concrete), and upholstery. Currently, because of laws created using lies, farmers in the U.S. are not allowed to grow industrial hemp, even though the U.S. is the world's number-one importer of hemp materials and hemp products. Allowing U.S. farmers to grow hemp would help them be more financially stable, give them another rotation crop to grow on polycrop farms, provide them with fuel (hemp oil can be used as fuel in diesel engines) and help the environment. Hemp does not require the use of toxic farming chemicals, and it produces more oxygen per acre than an acre of trees, while absorbing more greenhouse gasses than an acre of trees. An acre of hemp produces more fabric per acre than an acre of cotton, and uses less water to do so. Hemp also doesn't require the toxic chemicals used to produce massive quantities of cotton. (Access VoteHemp.com. Also see my book *Marijuana & Hemp: History, Uses, Laws, and Controversy.*)

IF YOU ARE NOT GROWING A FOOD GARDEN...

YOU are completely reliant on a food system that can collapse within a day. Do you think that is wise?

Most people are now living that way, with absolutely no idea what they would do for food if stores and restaurants shut down, such as if there were a problem with the banking system, electrical grid, or transportation and shipping systems.

Find a place to grow food. Your lawn. With a neighbor. Your patio or on a rooftop. A greenhouse. A community garden plot. An abandoned lot. Parks. Wildland.

Humans are reliant on Nature for nourishment. Most now give corporate stores and restaurants the middleman position between interacting with Nature, in exchange for money, which corporations use to formulate laws. Why are you giving them power by giving them your money?

Grow food!

Growing food is participating in the most basic and ancient way of interacting with Earth. Harvesting, eating, and then returning substances to the Earth through defecation and composting to create rich soil for growing more food is about as basic as you can get. If you find a way to do it without using money or being reliant on corporations or government, more power to you!

Stop allowing corporations to take away your basic relationship with Nature. Grow food. It's smart, nutritious, sustainable, less expensive, and saves time and energy.

ONE SOLUTION for all:
- To lower your food costs and boost energy...
- To improve your nutrition and get vitamin D...

- To reduce risk of cancer and other diseases...
- To reduce exposure to toxic chemicals: pesticides, miticides, and fungicides...
- To avoid irradiated food and food additives...
- To stop supporting companies involved in genetically modifying food plants...
- To use fewer fossil fuels and other resources...
- To reduce dependence on foreign oil...
- To become more self-sufficient...
- To build local culture and help your family...
- To reduce air, water, and soil pollution...
- To reconnect with Nature and help wildlife...
- To stop depending on the store and restaurant food distribution system that can collapse in one day – and leave you and your family hungry...

PLANT AND MAINTAIN A FOOD GARDEN, and compost your food scraps into soil using compost pits.

Compost pits are where you bury your food scraps one or more times per week. It is easier than a compost pile or compost bin. Dig a hole, burry. The food scraps then decompose and make the soil richer. You can also look up humanure and learn how to incorporate your own waste into creating rich gardening soil.

There are many people and organizations involved in the organic gardening movement. There are likely some active organic gardening groups within your town or city. Find them and get busy.

Bioneers, Bioneers.org
California Rare Fruit Growers, CRFG.org
Fallen Fruit, FallenFruit.org
Tilth, Tilth.org
Food Not Lawns, FoodNotLawns.com
Organic Gardening, OrganicGardening.com
United Plant Savers, UnitedPlantSavers.org
Kitchen Gardeners International, KGI.org
Yards to Gardens, Y2G.org;

Urban Homestead, UrbanHomestead.org
John Kohler, OKRaw.com
Seed Savers, SeedSavers.org
Victory Seeds, VictorySeeds.com
Urban Organic Gardening, UrbanOrganicGardener.com
United Plant Savers, UnitedPlantSavers.org

KITCHENS

KITCHENS can be interesting places. Gathering people and making food together for a feast is one way to nurture friends and family, and create community. Throughout human history this is often how food was made with neighbors, friends, and generations of families creating and sharing food. Eventually more and more single-family dwellings were built, each having a kitchen. With this change, the communal eating events became much less common. Traditions in food making were lost and more people began to rely on manufactured food. Instead of dinners shared by many people it became common for people to eat alone.

Now, when people want to eat with other people, they head to restaurants, where people aren't treated as equals, but as the served, the servers, and the backroom workers. It is one more step away from communicating with commonality.

Single kitchens are a stagnating force in human relations. It would be nice and less wasteful if more people shared their food-making skills and ate meals together while communicating their experiences about life.

Rich, poor, dark, light, old, young, bookish, artistic, philosophical, liberal, conservative, diverse genders, or whatever, a thing we have in common is that we need nourishment.

It is fun to invite people over and get busy creating food that may be for one meal, or that might last for several days, and that will bring groups of people together for sit-down social meals. I have either organized or been to many such feasts. No two have been alike and each brings the opportunity for building community, life-long friendships, healing to wounded relationships, and matching up of lovers.

Having access to a functional kitchen is key to creating many of the best foods. While sharing kitchens with others can be beneficial in many ways, creating a kitchen doesn't have to be expensive. Many kitchen tools, utensils, thingamajigs, and serving doohickeys can be bought secondhand at garage sales, in secondhand shops, and through community bulletin boards.

Dining tables don't have to be elaborate. I was at a dinner party where the table wasn't big enough, so we took a door from its hinges and jacked that up on wooden boxes to create a dining table.

Rather than having conformity in color and design, it can be more interesting to have plates, bowls, glasses, and eating utensils that are mismatched. Make the table look as diverse and eclectic as the people gathered to eat.

KITCHEN EQUIPMENT

MANY of these items can be purchased at secondhand stores. Also, check the community board at your local natural foods store. Others may have to be purchased new (such as chefs' knives).

Our oven sits as a relic of ancient times, and is used as a storage cabinet. Sometimes it is used to heat water. We have no use for toasters, ovens, broilers, grills, fryers, woks, or microwaves.

Asian or kimchi (also spelled *kim-chee*) crock: For making kimchi and sauerkraut. Get one and learn how to use it. Asian markets often sell them. Another possibility is a Harsch crock made by a company in Germany. Raw fermented foods made from organic produce are nutrient rich. I got mine from a neighbor who was moving away.

Bin with cover for kitchen scraps to be composted. Please compost! It is good to create your own garden soil.

Bamboo sushi roller. Can be used for creating a number of interesting food presentations.

Blender: There are a variety of blenders on the market. However, a strong, restaurant-quality blender is great for making all sorts of things, from hummus to sauces, and smoothies. The VitaMix brand blender with manual speed control knobs is pretty common in raw vegan kitchens. This requires an investment (presently about $400 to $500). I have seen Vitamix blenders for sale on the community bulletin board at the local natural foods store.

A Blendtec blender is also one that is used by a lot of raw foodists.

For those who don't have electricity in their living space, there is at least one company that makes a hand-crank blender. There is another that makes a solar blender.

Bowls: You need a variety of bowls. Stick with those that are made of glass, ceramic, and wood. Stay away from aluminum, plastic, and bowls that can rust, degrade, or release chemicals as food is soaking or stored in them.

Casserole dish. Glass casserole dishes can be used for a number of dishes, and also for sprouting and germinating seeds.

Champion juicer: Often used a lot.

Save the pulp from the vegetables you juice, mix them with flax seeds, and or hemp seeds; mix in some Himalayan sea salt (or not), minced garlic, diced onion, chopped tomatoes, or scissor-cut pieces of dried tomatoes, chopped Italian herbs, soaked seeds of pumpkin, sesame, and/or sunflower; mix in some nutritional yeast (or not), then spread on your dehydrator sheets, and dehydrate at about 108° for 24 hours (less or more depending on your desired level of crispness). Cut into squares and store in a cool place in a big glass jar. Use for dips, spreads, guacamole and other recipes from raw vegan recipe books.

Chef knives. A sharpening stone is also essential.

Citrus juicer: A mechanical juicer is a basic. A small, hand-held juicer can be useful if you only need to squeeze the juice from one lemon or other citrus fruit.

Citrus zester. For scraping orange and lemon peel for use in different dishes, or as garnish.

Coffee grinder: Used to grind cacao, flax seeds, pumpkin seeds, hemp seeds, herbs, etc.

Colanders

Crystal stones to keep in water bottles. Set your water bottles in the sun to solarize your water.

Cuisinart, or other food processor.

Cuisinart mini prep: For making salad dressings and sauces.

Cutting boards made of bamboo. Keep them dry and clean. Don't use soap on them.

Dehydrator, or a solar food dryer. If you purchase an electric dehydrator, seek out one that has an adjustable heat control. I tend to stay away from dehydrated foods because they make me feel dehydrated. But a dehydrator is useful for making vegetable crackers out of pulp left over from juicing vegetables. They are also handy for making seed and nut cheeses, pizza crust, granola, piecrusts, and raw vegan nut cheesecake crusts. They can always be used to dehydrate tomatoes and other soft fruits and vegetables for winter storage. Chefs I know are constantly making all sorts of experimental foods in their dehydrators. Some taste good. Some do not. Probably my favorite dehydrated food item is rawmasean that is made right, which involves several days to make rejuvelac from sprouted wheat berries, then blending the rejuvelac with soaked pignolis (pine nuts), mixing this with nutritional yeast (not brewers' yeast), and letting this ferment covered with a cloth for a day in a warm/dark place before adding Italian herbs and salt. Then, spreading on dehydrator sheets and dehydrating for a day at low heat. But, this is fattening, so… eat sparingly.

Funnel

Garden: The vast majority of people in so-called "civilized society" are completely reliant on supermarkets and corporate restaurants selling foods saturated with toxic substances. It is no wonder there are so many pharmacies and hospitals, and the airwaves are filled with commercials for prescription medications and over-the-counter drugs. Do yourself a favor and plant a food garden so you grow at least some of your food. Get relatives, neighbors, and friends to grow food gardens – and share in the bounty. Support regional organic farmers. Learn about wild edible plants. Disconnect from synthetic foods and drugs. Health does not come in a can or a pill.

Garlic press. I rarely use this item. I put the garlic on a cutting board, place the side of the chef's knife on top of it, and hit the knife. The garlic breaks open and splinters. The skin is then easy to remove, and makes for an easy way to dice the garlic.

117

Ginger grater: Made of porcelain.

Grater and shredder

Green Star juicer: Used much less often. I've heard others say that this is their favorite juicer. The one in my kitchen hardly gets used.

Icing bag: This can be used for decorating foods with creams and sauces.

Jars: Big glass ones for making herbal sun teas; making and refrigerating rejuvelac; storing seeds; sprouting; storing dehydrated foods; making wine (don't ask!); solarizing water, etc.

Juicer, such as a Champion or Green Star, or both, and a citrus juicer. About juicers: There are juicing machines that are favored above others, but it seems to be a matter of taste and function. I am more into making smoothies than juicing. With smoothies you get the nutrients that are also in the cell walls, which include antioxidants, biophotons, minerals, amino acids, and other beneficial substances. The Champion juicer here gets used a whole lot more than the Green Star juicer. Many people use a Champion juicer to make banana ice cream (simply put frozen bananas [peel them before freezing] through the blender using the solid plate, not the screen). But, we make banana whip ice cream using our Cuisinart, which we think works better.

Kimchi crock

Knife sharpener. We use a fine stone.

Knives: Professional chef quality. Chef's knife, paring knife, serrated knife, cleaver (for opening coconuts).

Mandolin: For cutting vegetables in fancy ways.

Measuring cups and spoons. I rarely use them. But a glass measuring cup often comes in handy.

Melon baller

Misting bottle containing hydrogen peroxide for misting produce before rinsing, and for sanitizing cutting boards and other surfaces (hydrogen peroxide breaks down into oxygen and water).

Mortar and pestle: Useful for making mustard, and for grinding seeds and fresh herbs. A bigger one is better than a smaller one.

Norwalk juicer: Some people swear these are the best juicers. I don't own one. They are expensive.

Peeler

Pie plates, glass.

Pitcher

Salad spinner: To spin rinsed greens free of water.

Scissors: A sturdy pair of kitchen scissors often comes in handy, especially for cutting herbs in the garden just before use, and for cutting up the herbs over various dishes. We also cut up the cilantro and parsley above the Cuisinart to then blend into spreads containing pulverized cilantro and/or parsley, lemon juice, red bell pepper, cumin, and sometimes nutritional yeast.

Screened shelf or box: Used to store fruits and vegetables, and to keep bugs away. Easy to create using a stapler or tacks on a small hinged door on a wooden box.

Screen strainers

Serving utensils: Triangular spatula, salad spoon and fork, tongs, soup ladle.

Shovel, for burying the kitchen scraps in a compost pit. We have several compost pits, where we bury the scraps, rather than using a compost pile. Pits attract worms and breed and nurture soil organisms. Compost piles and tumblers attract flies and smell.

Shredder

Solar power panel on the roof or in the yard for creating electricity. Or, a bird-safe wind turbine.

Spatulas

Spice grater

Spiralizer/Saladacco: For making zucchini "pasta."

Spoons: Metal, ceramic, and wooden. A small wooden spoon, or a ceramic spoon, is good to use in honey (for those that use honey) and miso (for those that use that fermented product).

Sprouter: Fresh Life Automatic Sprouter, or Biosta tiered sprouter, or other sprouter. You can also use a large jar, or glass casserole with clear glass cover.

We like to use glass jars and glass casserole dishes rather than plastic sprouters because plastic can leach toxins into the food.

We don't own a mechanized sprouter. Some people like them. But, if you can use less electricity, why not do that instead?

Strainers: Both hand held mesh strainers and bowl-type strainers with legs are useful. Another way of straining water out of salad is a salad spinner, or by spreading salad on a towel, and gently rolling the towel into a roll to absorb water.

Steamer basket or double boiler: For those wishing to steam vegetables at low heat.

Sushi roller, bamboo. Can be used for making a variety of foods.

Torte pans: These are two-piece pie pans that come in a variety of depths and sizes for creating freestanding cakes, pies, tarts, and tortes.

Towels: There is always something that is in need of drying, wiping, or cleaning. Cleanliness in food preparation is a very good thing. Organic cotton is good, but hemp towels will last longer because the fibers are sturdier. Don't worry about getting them stained, because they will get stained. Once they are too old to use in the kitchen they can be used for household cleaning. They can easily be cleaned in a big bowl with some biodegradable dish soap, and hung out in sun to dry. If they are 100 percent natural fiber, such as cotton or hemp (no polyester or other plastic fiber), they can eventually be cut up and tossed into the compost pit. Avoid using paper towels; we don't need to be cutting down our forests to throw them away.

Vegetable peeler

Wheat grass sprouter and juicer

KITCHEN FOOD STOCK

"Either is it is appropriable material for tissue building – a food, or it is not. If not, then it is a foreign substance – a poison – and as such can only damage and cannot possibly ever benefit the organism."

– Dr. Hereward Carrington

THERE are a number of companies specializing in quality, organic foods common in raw food kitchens.

There are a lot of choices to be made with how and what to use when making food.

Some people avoid certain ingredients, such as gluten, bottled oils, salt, agave, spices, and other ingredients, while others don't seem to share the same concerns or issues.

Some raw foodists avoid salt. I usually don't use salt in the foods I make. But, when I'm at a restaurant or a dinner party, I'm not opposed to eating foods containing salt. If I know something has a lot of salt, I usually avoid it. I have found that the longer I stay away from salty foods, the stronger and less pleasant the taste of salt becomes.

Some people will use agave as a sweetener, but others avoid it. I mostly avoid it, don't purchase it, but will sometimes eat foods containing agave if I'm at a raw restaurant, at a dinner party, or otherwise eating foods made by someone else. I don't like the overly processed sugar taste that agave has. It is simply another junk sweetener, and is not a health food.

Some people that are otherwise raw, will use maple syrup, while others consider maple syrup to be a cooked food, and they avoid it. (Maple syrup is the sap of the maple tree that has been slowly simmered into syrup.) I am not opposed to maple syrup, but I also don't often use it. I love the flavor of it, and would rather not have it around.

Other sweeteners raw foodists may use include dates, coconut sap or coconut sap sugar; raisins; figs; or paste made from dates or raisins or figs (soaked raisins, dates, or figs placed in a food processor with a little bit of the soaking water, and then combined/processed into a paste), yacon syrup, stevia, or raw honey. Some people avoid honey, and other bee products, such as bee pollen and royal jelly. I usually avoid honey and bee products.

Some people will eat raw chocolate, and some people avoid it, and may use raw carob instead. I mostly avoid chocolate, and prefer carob. Many of the companies claiming to sell raw chocolate are selling chocolate that has been heat processed. I don't consider chocolate to be some wonder food, as many people do. I think the biggest benefit of chocolate is to the people who are selling it. Maybe you are one who believes the hype you hear about the benefits of eating raw chocolate, which is your choice. I don't believe it is good for the adrenal glands or nerves, and many people agree with me. Chocolate does contain addictive and neurotoxic substances, can cause rapid heartbeat, can interfere with sleep, and may contribute to anxiety, stress, mood swings, and energy dips. Most people who ever lived never had chocolate, and it is not a necessary ingredient in the human diet.

Some people use lemon instead of vinegar in their dressings. Some people don't use vinegar in or on anything. I'll use either, but prefer fresh lemon.

Some people use nama shoyu, while others avoid it because it contains gluten. I avoid foods containing nama shoyu.

At Living Light Culinary Institute, Cherie Soria's recipes don't contain vinegar or nama shoyu.

Some raw vegan restaurants use Coconut Secret, a 100% organic, raw coconut amino, and no longer use tamari or nama shoyu. More and more raw restaurants and food companies have also stopped using agave, and use coconut sap and other sweeteners instead.

You may notice on packaged raw food labels wording stating, "Does not contain nama shoyu or agave." Raw food companies are becoming aware of how many people are avoiding those ingredients.

One thing is certain, and that is: raw foodies are true foodies, and they are always experimenting with varieties of organic fruits, vegetables, nuts, seeds, seaweeds, and flowers to find what they like, what is more nutritious, what doesn't cause adverse reactions, and what can be combined with other foods to create satisfying tastes and textures. If you think you know the world of raw food, wait a year or two, and you will likely have a lot more to learn.

The best foods you can have in the kitchen are those you grow organically yourself with soil enriched by kitchen compost, and also those you get from local organic farmers. Research organic gardening. My book, *Sunfood Traveler: Global Guide to Raw Food Culture*, contains a lot of information about groups promoting organic home gardening, community gardening, and wild food harvesting.

If you have a food co-op nearby, it is good to join so that you can get discounts on organic foods. Co-ops typically purchase in bulk, and share the discount with members. You can get extra discounts on foods that you can purchase by the case. If there isn't a co-op near you, consider starting one.

You may be able to purchase in bulk from an organic wholesaler, such as those wholesalers in the downtown of a large city. These are the companies that import fruits and vegetables, or buy truckloads of them from local organic farms, and sell them to stores and restaurants. Your local natural foods store produce worker may be able to tell you the names of the local companies from which they are purchasing their fruits and vegetables.

It is also good to have a variety of organic seeds for germinating or sprouting. Germinated seeds and sprouts contain more nutrients than the ungerminated seeds. Adding germinated seeds and sprouts to your diet is a low-cost way to keep a variety of nutrients in your daily diet. Typically, in my kitchen, there are a variety of jars of germinates and sprouts going at the same time – using one jar of sprouts every day, and starting a new one. For more information on sprouting, see my book, *Sunfood Traveler: Global Guide to Raw Food Culture*.

Blessed Herbs, Oakham, MA, USA, BlessedHerbs.com. For organic herbs.

Bautista Family Organic Date Ranch, POB 726, Mecca, CA 92254-0726; 760-396-2337

Council for Responsible Genetics, 5 Upland Rd., Ste. 3, Cambridge, MA 02140; CouncilForResponsibleGenetics.org. Founded in 1983, the CRG is comprised of scientists, lawyers, public health advocates, and citizens concerned about the social, ethical, and environmental impact of new genetic technologies. They have influenced a group of seed companies to sign a "safe seed pledge," committing to preserving the integrity of seeds from genetic engineering. For a list of the seed companies that have signed the pledge, please contact the Council.

Fat Uncle Farms, California; FUncleFarms.blogspot.com. Raw almonds.

Frontier Natural Products Co-op, Iowa; FrontierCoop.com. Sells sprouting supplies.

Handy Pantry, Utah; HandyPantry.com. Sprouting supplies.

Heirloom Organics, Sprouting-Seeds.com.

Living Light Culinary Institute, RawFoodChef.com. Cherie Soria's raw chef institute sells a variety of kitchen gadgets for raw food prep.

Mendocino Sea Vegetable Company, POB 455, Philo, CA 95466; Seaweed.net

Mountain Rose Herbs, Eugene, OR; MountainRoseHerbs.com. Sells herbs and sprouting supplies.

Mumm's Sprouting Seeds, Saskatchewan, Canada; Sprouting.com.

Selina Naturally, Arden, NC, USA; CelticSeaSalt.com. Markets unprocessed salts.

Sprout House, New York; SproutHouse.com.

Sprout People, San Francisco, CA; SproutPeople.com. Sells organic sprouting seeds.

UB Raw, ubraw.com/rawtools.html. Sells a scraping and peeling tool for creating noodles out of coconut or zucchini. It was created by Minh Skurow. She, and her husband, Ron, teach about raw food and hold raw food recipe classes.

RECIPE BOOKS

IT is good to eat simply. Instead of always working to make every meal into a gourmet feast, make some meals into monomeals. By that, I mean eating only one thing during a meal: such as eating a melon, or eating several tangerines, or eating a few mangoes, or a big bowl of strawberries, including the leaves (yes, the leaves of strawberries contain a variety of nutrients).

Get into making green smoothies. These are made by blending water, some fruit, and some green leafy vegetables. When you make them, don't make them too thick, but do include a good bit of water. Also, if you have access to chia seeds, toss a teaspoon of those into the smoothie as they will help give you a full feeling while increasing the omega-3 fatty acids. Avoid guzzling green smoothies, drinking massive amounts of them, or relying on them too heavily. Rather, drink slowly, savoring their flavor and allowing the digestive juices of your mouth to begin the conversion process.

Learn to make salads from scratch, including the dressings – especially from foods you grow in a home garden. Doing so will be more healthful, and save money.

For variety, once-in-a-while, go for it, and make some of your favorite gourmet raw foods, pimped-out salads, and luscious raw desserts.

There are a growing number of raw recipe books. But, look for those that are lower in fat, and that don't use agave, nama shoyu, or a lot of salt, oil, or nuts. Skate boarder and yogi Chris Kendall has published a helpful booklet of low fat raw vegan recipes titled *101 Fricken' Rawsome Recipes* (Access: TheRawAdvantage.com) Veronica Grace Patenaude has produced a low fat raw vegan recipe DVD that is accompanied by a booklet. Megan Elizabeth has also produced low fat raw vegan recipe books that she sells on her site (Access: MeganElizabeth.com/books). Kristina Carillo-Bucaram, who founded the Rawfully Organic Food Co-op in Houston, features low fat raw vegan recipes on her site (Access: FullyRaw.com).

If you are on the Internet, see Dara Dubinet's YouTube channel. Dara demonstrates some low fat raw, gourmet raw, or mostly raw recipes.

See the book about raw food nutrition, *Becoming Raw: The Essential Guide to Raw Vegan Diets*, by Brenda Davis, Vesanto Melina, and Rynn Berry. I wouldn't advise using the nama shoyu that some of the recipes in the book contain. A better choice may be to use coconut aminos, which are becoming more common in healthfood stores. Also, instead of chocolate, use carob.

Use dates, coconut bud sap, coconut sugar crystals, or maple syrup instead of agave. Agave is NOT a healthfood. Raw honey would be a lesser choice, and only for those who use honey. Dates can be used as a sweetener, or soak dates in water, then blend the dates with the soak water to create date paste.

Cut the oil in recipes in half, or a fourth, or maybe, depending on the recipe, avoid adding the oil altogether. You may find that you like foods better without the oil. If you are an athlete, you may find your endurance improves by avoiding foods containing bottled oils, and by avoiding consuming many nuts.

Brenda Davis and Vesanto Melina are also the co-authors with Cherie Soria of *Raw Food Revolution Diet*. Davis and Melina got into raw foods while researching and helping Cherie Soria write *Raw Food Revolution*, then they wrote the book, *Becoming Raw*.

For athletic performance, read *Thrive Fitness: Mental and Physical Strength for Life*, by Brendan Brazier. He also wrote the *Thrive Diet*. Also, consider Douglas Graham's book, *The 80/10/10 Diet*. For a broader understanding on health and nutrition, read *The China Study*, by T. Colin Campbell, and

Prevent and Reverse Heart Disease, by Caldwell Esselstyn. Also, read books by Dr. Neal Barnard (Access: NealBarnard.org) and Dr. John McDougall (Access: DrMcDougall.com).

RANDOM RECIPES FOR A RAW VEGAN KITCHEN

For more recipes, access:
DaraDubinet.com
Megan Elizabeth, MeganElizabeth.com
Elaina Love's Pure Joy Planet, PureJoyPlanet.com
Living-foods.com/recipes/
Goneraw.com/recipes
RawFoodChef.com
Rawmazing.com/rawmazing-recipes/

SALADS

• SIMPLE SALAD

In a large bowl, combine:
Half of a head of **Romain lettuce or one-half bunch kale**, finely chopped
Juice of one-half **lemon**
One ripe **avocado**, pitted, skinned, and finely cut into cubes
Palm full **pine nuts or fractured walnuts**

Optional:
Several **grape tomatoes**
Spoonfull **black currants**
Two pinches **salt** (optional)
One diced **pear or peach**
Ground **black pepper**
Freshly chopped herbs: **oregano or basil**

• KALE SALAD BASICS

Base:
Destem the kale leaves.
Dice the kale.

Dressing:
Lemon juice

Coconut sugar or a couple of dates blended into a few tablespoons of **water**
Hemp oil, or no oil
Dijon mustard, or not
A few pinches of **dulse flakes**, or not
Salt, or no salt

Optional:
Include two or more of the following fruit:
Blueberries
Thinly sliced **strawberries**
Cherry or grape tomatoes, or diced dried tomatoes
Apple, diced
Pieces of **mandarin orange**
Diced **mango**
Black **currants or raisins**
Grapes
Goji berries
Green olives, diced
Diced avocado

Include one or ore of the following vegetables:
Thin slices of **celery**
Red bell pepper, diced
Chopped **cucumber**

Include one or more of the seeds or nuts:
Raw **pumpkin seeds**
Sunflower seeds
Sesame seeds
Hemp seeds
Millet, raw
Fractured **walnuts**
Fractured **pecans**
Fractured **macadamia nuts**

Fractured **Brazil nuts**

Include one or more herbs and spices:
Italian **parsley**, diced
Oregano
Cilantro, diced
Sage
Dill
Rosemary
Black pepper
Cayenne pepper powder

• SIMPLE KALE SALAD

Soak in water for about a half hour:
One-half cup **sundried tomatoes** finely chopped
One-half cup **pinenuts**

While the above is soaking in water, prepare the following:
One bunch of **kale**, finely chopped
One or two shredded **carrots**
A dozen or so **grape tomatoes**
One medium **red onion**, sliced thinly
Several raw **olives**, sliced
Juice of one **lemon**
Two tablespoons raw **hemp or olive oil**
A little **salt or dulse** powder (optional)
A tablespoon of **coconut aminos**

Strain:
The water out of the pinenuts and tomatoes

Toss all ingredients together in a bowl. Chill and serve.

• KALE SALAD FOR FOUR

In a large bowl, combine:
Two bunches of finely chopped **kale**
Two diced **Roma tomatoes**
Several fractured **walnuts**
Eight raw **green olives**, diced
One-fourth of a **red onion**, diced
One-forth of a **red bell pepper**, diced
Two cored, unpeeled **apples**, diced
One-fourth cup **raisins**
Two tablespoons **nutritional yeast** (not brewer's yeast)
One tablespoon **millet** (not heated)
One tablespoon **sesame seeds**
Two tablespoons fractured **hemp seeds**

Dressing:
In food processor, combine:
Three or four **dates**
Juice from one half **lemon**
Tablespoon prepared **mustard** (such as Dijon)
Teaspoon **hemp seed oil** (or no oil)
Teaspoon **dill**
Teaspoon **thyme**
Half a teaspoon **chili powder**
Two tablespoons **water**

Optional:
Half a teaspoon vegan **probiotic powder**
Dash of **cayenne** powder
Dash of **salt** (optional)

One diced **peach**
Several diced **strawberries**
Handful **blueberries**

• FANCY KALE SALAD

Toss in a big salad bowl:
Two bunches of **kale**, finely chopped
Two **Roma tomatoes**, sliced to bits
Several raw **walnuts**, fractured
Eight **green olives**, diced (unless you can't find raw olives)
One-fourth **red onion**, diced
One-fourth **red bell pepper**, diced
Two **apples**, diced (black Arkansas or apples of your choice)
A palm-full of **raisins or cranberries**
One-half cup of **nutritional yeast** (unless avoiding nutritional yeast)
A tablespoon or two of raw, unheated **millet** seeds
A tablespoon or two of raw **sesame seeds**
A tablespoon or two of raw **hemp seeds**
One teaspoon **probiotic powder**
One tablespoon **thyme**
One teaspoon **dill**
A couple of dashes of **cayenne powder** (unless avoiding cayenne)
Two tablespoons **spirulina powder**

Dressing:
In a Cuisinart, combine:
Four **dates**
Two or three tablespoons of **stone ground or Dijon**

mustard
Juice of one-half **lemon** (or more)
Two tablespoons **apple cider vinegar**
Two tablespoons **hemp oil or flax oil**
One tablespoon **water**

Toss together. Chill.

• EINSTEIN SALAD

This salad is a rather involved salad that is
particularly rich in brain and bone nutrients. It's a great
salad for bringing to dinner parties and holidays.

All ingredients raw, unheated, and organically grown.

Presoak the following greens
In one-half cup lemon juice and one-half teaspoon salt
for an hour or so, or half day in a covered bowl in the
refrigerator. To get the leaves coated with the lemon
juice and salt, mix them with your hands. Some people
purposely squish the leaves as they do this, and this is
why you may hear people describe this is a "massaged
salad":
One-half cup finely chopped **chard or kale**
One-half cup finely chopped **broccoli**
One-half cup finely chopped **celery**
One-half cup finely chopped **dandelion greens**
One-half cup finely chopped **Italian parsley**
One-half cup finely chopped **collard greens**

(You can also use spinach, beet greens, or other greens)

After soaking, put in strainer and lightly rinse with water. Spin dry in salad spinner. If you don't have a spinner, spread the rinsed greens on a clean towel, and gently roll to absorb the majority of water.

Soak:
One tablespoon **mustard seeds** in water for about half a day
One-fourth cup **sunflower seeds** in water for 4 to 8 hours

Put into big bowl: the salad mix above with:
One-fourth cup chopped **raw walnuts**
One-fourth cup raw **sunflower seeds** (soaked)
One chopped **apple**
One finely chopped red or **yellow bell pepper**
One-fourth cup fresh **pomegranate seeds or raisins or currants**
One cubed **avocado** (pitted and peeled)

Dressing: blend together:
One tablespoon **mustard seeds** (good to soak in a water first)
One clove **garlic**, minced
Six raw **olives**, pitted, chopped
Nine raw, fresh **cranberries, or** about 15 **fresh blueberries**
One-fourth cup **hemp oil** or cold-pressed grapeseed oil, or olive oil
One teaspoon minced fresh **ginger root**
Tiny pinch of **red pepper**
One tablespoon **nutritional yeast** (optional)
One teaspoon **spirulina**
One-fourth teaspoon pink or sea **salt** (optional)

One tablespoon freshly ground **flax seeds** (use coffee grinder)
Juice from half an **orange**, or three to four tablespoons apple juice

Optional:
One to two tablespoons of raw **honey or maple syrup**

Toss the salad and dressing together. Chill.

• VOONA SALAD

This is a good dinner party salad.

In a LARGE bowl, toss in:
Palm full of soaked raw **sunflower seeds**
Palm full of fractured raw **walnuts** (optional)
One bunch of **kale**, de-ribbed and chopped fine
One bunch **spinach or chard**, chopped fine
Two ribs of **celery**, chopped fine
One **red bell pepper**, chopped fine
One half **red onion**, diced
One or two **Roma tomatoes**, cut into small cubes, or a dozen grape tomatoes cut in half
One ripe large **avocado**, cut into small cubes
Handful of chopped **cranberries** or whole **blueberries** or **fresh pomegranate seeds** (all optional)
Dashes of **black pepper** to taste
One teaspoon of **pink salt or sea salt** (optional)
One tablespoon diced fresh **thyme** and/or **basil**
Dashes of **cayenne pepper** to taste (optional)
One-half teaspoon **dulse powder or flakes**
Two tablespoons **dill**
Handfull chopped **Italian parsley** and/or **cilantro**

Sprinkle of raw **millet** or **hemp seeds** (optional)
A dozen chopped **black or green olives** (optional)

Dressing: One-half cup (or a little more) of oil-free **raw hummus** made of:

 1½ Cups two-day germinated **garbanzo beans**
  [soak ¾ Cup dried garbanzos overnight, then rinse
  and strain two or three times per day for two days]

 ¼ Cup diced **sundried tomatoes** soaked for half hour
  in 2 Tablespoons **apple cider vinegar**

**Blend the germinated garbanzoes and soaked
sundried tomatoes in a high-speed blender with:**

¼ Cup freshly squeezed **lemon juice**
3 to 4 Tablespoons organic **tahini**
4 to 6 cloves **garlic** diced
1 level teaspoon **paprika**
1 level teaspoon **turmeric**
Salt to taste (optional)

After tossing together, chill before serving. Garnish with
grapes and/or slices of apples or pears.

• SLIVER SALAD

Key to this salad is to use a mandolin, or a food
processor with the shredding blade. The last option
would be to slice all very fine with a sharp chef's knife.

Shred:
One large or two medium-sized **carrots**
One 2" slice of a **daikon radish**
One **parsnip**
One **red bell pepper**
One **turnip**
Put all shredded veggies into a large salad bowl.

Stir in:
One finely chopped **shallot**
Two finely chopped **scallions**
One palmful finely chopped **Italian parsley**
One cup chopped **lettuce** of your choice
One cup finely sliced **black kale**
One finely chopped rib of **celery**
One cup finely chopped **cucumber**
Handful of fresh **sunflower sprouts**

Toss in:
One tablespoon **dulse** flakes or powder
One tablespoon **millet**
Half a teaspoon **black pepper**
One-fourth cup **shredded almonds**
Fresh squeezed juice of half a **lemon** (or one lime)
One tablespoon **hemp seed oil**

Serve chilled.

Optional:
If you prefer it to be sweet, add a couple of tablespoon of raw **honey**. Or, finely chop three or four **dates**, soak them in half a cup of water, then add these to the salad with a little bit of the soak water. Garnish with organically grown **edible flower**.

• CARROT FENNEL SALAD

By Rose Lee Calabro, author of the recipe book *Living in the Raw*

In a jar, combine, cover, and shake:
Four tablespoons fresh **lemon juice**

Two tablespoons cold-pressed **flax oil**
One-half teaspoon **Celtic sea salt** (optional)

In a large bowl, combine:
Six **carrots**, finely sliced
Six sprigs of **mint**
Four green **onions**, chopped
One **fennel bulb**, finely sliced

Pour dressing over the salad mix, toss gently, chill, and serve.

• CUCUMBER SALAD

With a fork:
Take four medium-sized **cucumbers** and score them lengthwise with the fork, creating grooves. Some people like to peel the cucumbers. Some don't.

With a chef knife:
Cut cucumbers in half lengthwise, then slice very thinly

Dice:
One peeled small to medium **red onion**
One-half cup **fresh dill**. If unable to obtain fresh dill, use about one-fourth cup dried dill.

Blend:
One-fourth cup **olive oil**
Juice from one **lemon**
One-fourth cup **apple vinegar**
Three peeled cloves of **garlic**
One teaspoon pink or **sea salt** (optional)

Place all together in a bowl, stir, chill.

Optional:
Top with a few cut olives and/or grapes.

Slice in half (either through the middle or top to bottom) and scrape out the seeds:
Six red bell peppers (in Australia they are called *capsicums*)

Fill the bell peppers with the mixture from the food processor. You can eat them straight away or dehydrate them at 115 degrees Fahrenheit for four hours.

Serves six.

• CORN SALAD

In a bowl, combine:
Kernels cut from one unheated cob of **corn**
Squeeze of one-forth **lemon**
Handful of fractured **cashews or macadamia nuts**
Heaping tablespoon raw **shredded coconut** meat
One **green onion**, diced
Palmfull of diced **cilantro**
One pinch **curry** powder

Optional:
Pinch of **salt**

• FETTUCCINI ALFREDO

Soak in water overnight:
One-and-a-half cups raw **macadamia nuts**
One small handful raw **walnuts**

To make fettuccini noodles, peel:
Three **zucchini**. Using the peeler, keep shaving the peeled zucchini to make long "noodles."

Strain:
The water from the macadamia and walnuts

To make Alfredo sauce, combine in food processor until smooth:
The **macadamia nuts**
The **walnuts**
Three cloves of fresh **garlic**
One-fourth cup cold-pressed, raw **olive oil or hemp seed oil**
Two teaspoons **black pepper**
Two teaspoons sea **salt** (optional)
Enough **water** to make the mixture into a thick sauce
Several raw **pinenuts** (optional)

In large bowl:
Pour the sauce into the bowl, then gently stir the zucchini fettuccini noodles into the sauce.

Chop:
Fresh **parsley and/or oregano**. Sprinkle on top of the fettuccini Alfredo as a garnish.

Optional:
Garnish with fresh **grapes**.

Dressings, Sauces, Salsa, Spreads, Marinara, Gravy

• Tahini Dressing

Combine in a blender:
One half cup raw organic **tahini**
One half cup freshly squeezed **lemon juice**
One or two cloves **garlic** peeled and minced
Big pinch **dulse powder**
One full teaspoon minced **white onion**
Water added by the tablespoon only until dressing reaches the desired consistency

Optional:
Salt to taste.

• Herbal Sunflower Cream Dressing

Soak in water for several hours:
One half cup **sunflower seeds**.

Drain and rinse the sunflowers. Place in sprouting jar, rinsing day and night for two days. Allowing them to germinate. On third day, place on towel allowing them to dry for several hours to half a day.

Using the S-blade in the food processor, combine until fine:
The germinated **sunflower seeds** with
One or two cloves of **garlic** crushed and diced
A large pinch of **dried basil**
A pinch of **thyme**
A pinch of **dulse flakes or kelp powder**

Add:
One or two tablespoons **lemon juice**
One or two tablespoons **hemp seed oil**
A few tablespoons **water**, and more if needed until the dressing reaches a creamy consistency

Optional:
Salt to taste.
Instead of basil and thyme, you can use **dill.**
If you are going to use the dressing right away, you can also add a thumb-sized piece of **avocado** as you are blending it.

• RANCH DRESSING

Soak in water for one hour and then drain the water:
One cup **macadamia nuts** or **cashews**

Blend until creamy smooth:
The **macadamia nuts or cashews**
One-fourth cup **lemon juice**
One-fourth cup **hemp oil or cold pressed organic olive oil**
One-inch piece of **cucumber**

A palm full of diced **chives**
Tablespoon of **rosemary**
Tablespoon of **sage**
Tablespoon of **oregano**
Water, only if needed, added by the tablespoon until
mixture is smooth

Optional:
Salt to taste
Dash of **dulse flakes**
Half teaspoon of **black pepper**
Two tablespoons of minced **white onion**
Dash of **paprika**
Instead of rosemary, sage, and oregano, add 2
tablespoons of **dill** and a tablespoon of minced **parsley**

Can be used as a dip or as a salad dressing.

Salad idea options:
chopped **romaine or iceberg lettuce**
chopped **kale or chard**
chopped **red bell pepper**
chopped **red onion**
slivered **cucumber**
diced **apple**
shredded **carrots**
raisins
croutons made of crumbled dehydrated seed crackers

• CREAMY AVOCADO DRESSING + SALAD

Combine in Cuisinart until creamy:

One (large or two small) **avocado,** peeled and pitted
Juice from an **orange**
Tablespoon **lime juice**
Optional to this mix:
One-half of a **green chili pepper,** seeded and diced
A few raw **walnuts**
Two or three tablespoons **hemp seed oil**
Several leaves of **purslane** weed

In bowl, mix the avocado, lime and orange mixture
with:
Half cup chopped **cilantro**
Black pepper to taste
One-fourth of a **white onion,** chopped

Optional:
Salt to taste, chopped **green onion,** dash of **dulse flakes.**

Use as a dressing for a salad made of
Chopped **Romaine or iceberg lettuce**
Shredded **beet**
Shredded **carrot**
Diced ½ cup **cucumber**
Diced **red bell pepper**

Optional:
Diced **scallion,** chopped **spinach,** diced **green olives,**
grape or **cherry tomatoes,** a few spoonfuls of **black currants,** palm full of fractured **raw walnuts,** palm full
of fractured raw **hemp seeds, sunflower seeds,
sprouts.**

Salad can also be used as a wrap in a **collard green.**

• CAESAR DRESSING

Soak in water for an hour:
In one bowl: One half cup raw **macadamia** nuts
In second bowl: one-forth cup raw **pine nuts**
In third bowl, two or three pitted raw **dates**

Drain and rinse the nuts and dates.

In a high-speed blender with tamper, combine:
The macadamia nuts, pine nuts, and dates with:
One large, peeled clove of **garlic**
One-fourth cup **coconut water**
Two or three **basil leaves**
Black pepper to taste

Optional:
Salt to taste. **Dulse** flakes. A squeeze of **lemon**.

Salad idea:
Romaine lettuce
Capers
Green olives
Croutons made of dehydrated vegetable pulp (left over from juicing vegetables), dill, pumpkin seeds, and, if desired, salt.

• APPLE-GRAPE VINAIGRETTE

Soak in water for about 30 to 60 minutes:
Two pitted **dates**

Drain the dates and, in a blender, combine:
One cup **apple cider vinegar**
Three tablespoons **coconut aminos**
One tablespoon **Dijon mustard**
One pinch of **dulse flakes**
One thumb-sized piece of ripe **avocado**
Several **green grapes**

Optional:
A pinch of **dill**

• CREAMY SALAD DRESSING

In high-speed blender, combine:
One-fourth cup **pine nuts**
Three tablespoons **apple vinegar**
Juice from one-half **lemon**
Three-fourths cup **hemp seed oil**
Three peeled cloves **garlic**
Palm full of fresh **basil**, or slightly smaller amount of dry basil
Sprig of fresh **oregano**, or one teaspoon dry oregano
One teaspoon pink or sea **salt** (optional)

Chill.

This is nice over a salad of **spinach, grape tomatoes,** thin slices of **cucumber,** and some diced bits of **dandelion greens.** Garnish with a sprinkle of **dill,** a dash of **nutritional yeast,** and some shredded **carrot.**

• COOL CILUMBER DRESSING

In a blender, combine until smooth:
One-half cup chopped fresh **cilantro**
Two inches of **cucumber**, chopped
One peeled and pitted large **avocado**
One or two cloves **garlic**, minced
Three or four tablespoons **lemon juice**
Two tablespoons **lime juice**
Three or four tablespoons **apple cider vinegar**
A few tablespoons **water**, until dressing meets desired consistency

Optional:
Pinch of **dulse flakes**
Salt to taste
Olive or hemp oil instead of water

• CITRUS-GINGER DRESSING

In high-speed blender, combine until creamy smooth:
One-fourth cup fresh **cilantro**, chopped
One-inch piece of fresh **ginger root**, diced
One-half of a small **shallot**, diced
About two-thirds cup fresh Thai **coconut water**
Full tablespoon of fresh **coconut meat** from Thai coconut
Inch-sized piece of **lemon peel**, diced
Juice from one **orange**
One **date**, pitted

Optional:
Four tablespoons **olive oil**
Salt to taste, or use dulse or kelp

Chill.

• ALMOND-GINGER DRESSING

Soak in water for an hour or two:
One-half cup raw **almonds**
Five **dates** (pits removed)

Drain the almonds and dates and blend with:
Four tablespoons raw **tahini**
Half thumb-sized piece of raw **ginger root**
One clove of **garlic**
Half a teaspoon of **vanilla**
Tablespoon **hemp seed powder**
Big pinch of **dulse flakes** (optional)
One cup **water***

* If more water is needed, add it by the tablespoon full
until desired consistency is reached.

• SIMPLE DRESSING

From Julie Tolentino, a private chef in California.
Julestolen (at) yahoo.com

This recipe can be made any time with just a few
ingredients. No blender or food processor necessary.

In a bowl, whisk together:
One-fourth cup **lemon juice**
One-teaspoon **agave or raw honey**
Pinch of sea **salt** or **dulse**
One-fourth cup of **olive oil**

Optional:
One teaspoon **balsamic vinegar**

The best thing about this dressing is you don't even have to measure out the ingredients after you have made it once. Simply add ingredients to a big bowl of mixed greens as you go. Amounts of each ingredient can vary depending on your taste buds. Simple enough to use on just about any green salad variation.

• ALFREDO SALAD DRESSING

Soak in water for half a day:
One and a half cups raw **sunflower seeds**
One and a half cups **pine nuts** (pignolis)

When the seeds and nuts are done soaking, pour into a screen strainer or colander to strain them and then mildly rinse under water.

Put the seeds and nuts into a blender, and combine with:
Juice of one large or two small **lemons**
Three or four cloves of **garlic**
Half a teaspoon of **black pepper**
Pinch of **kelp powder**

Enough **water** to get the consistency of thick salad dressing.

When done blending, pour into bowl and taste. If **salt** is desired, add salt and stir until desired taste is accomplished.

Chill.

Optional:
Some people add a tablespoon of **nutritional yeast** to this mix.

• CHUNKY CORN SALSA

In a large bowl, stir together:
Six ears of **corn**, slice off the corn with sharp knife
One-half **red bell pepper**, diced
One-half **yellow bell pepper**, diced
Three medium to large **tomatoes**, diced
One-fourth cup **chives**, diced
One-half cup diced **cilantro**
One tablespoon fresh **lemon juice**

Optional, one or more of the following:
One clove **garlic**, crushed and diced
One tablespoon **olive or hemp oil**
One teaspoon **cumin powder**
Salt to taste (optional)
Black pepper to taste
A few pinches **cayenne powder**

In blender:
Take one cup of the salsa and blend until creamy.

Pour the one cup of blended salsa in with the rest of the salsa and mix well. Chill.

• FRESH TOMATO SALSA
From Matt Amsden of RawVolution
Access: RawVolution.com

In a mixing bowl, stir together:
Two cups chopped **tomatoes**
Three-fourth cup chopped **cilantro**
One-half cup chopped **yellow onions or scallions**
Two tablespoons fresh **lemon or lime juice**
One tablespoon **olive oil**
Four cloves **garlic**, minced
One-fourth teaspoon **cayenne powder**
Three-fourths teaspoon (or less) **sea salt**
One and one-half teaspoon ground **cumin**
Three-fourth teaspoon ground **coriander**

• NAISE SPREAD

This is one raw vegan version of mayonnaise.

Soak in water for one to three hours, then drain:
One cup raw cashews

In a high-speed blender, combine:
The soaked **cashews**
One or two pitted **dates**

Juice of one **lemon**
A thumb-sized slice of **brown onion**
One peeled clove of **garlic**
Two tablespoons **hemp oil**
Two tablespoons **olive or flax oil**
One pinch of **white pepper**
One pinch **dulse powder**
One teaspoon pink or **sea salt** (optional)
A little **water**, just enough to make the naise the consistency you desire.

Chill.

• SUNDRIED TOMATO BUTTER

From Anand and Runi of Raw Power Australia,
LiveFoodEducation.com

In a high speed blender, blend into almost a powder:
Eight **sun-dried tomatoes**
Add the rest of the ingredients, and blend until smooth, using the tamper to fully blend all ingredients.
One large **avocado** (large)
One tablespoon **tamari**
One-half clove of **garlic** (optional)
Two teaspoons **parsley** (optional)

This is a yummy vegan butter alternative and is delicious on flax crackers and raw breads. Alternatively, you can use it any savory recipe where you'd normally use butter.

• MATBOUKHA

By Maya Melamed of ChangingMaya.com.au, in Sydney, Australia.
Moroccan style red capsicum relish.

In a Cuisinart or food processor, combine the following until completely smooth:
One and a half cups **sun dried tomatoes**
One cup seeded chopped **tomatoes**
One-half red hot **chili pepper**
One-eighth teaspoon **cayenne pepper**
One-fourth teaspoon sweet **paprika**
One teaspoon **garlic powder**
One-fourth cup **olive oil**

Dice:
Two **red bell peppers**, chopped
One-half **green bell pepper**, chopped

Place in serving bowl and combine the diced bell peppers with the other ingredients. Chill.

Serve with dehydrated veggie and/or seed **crackers**, coin slices of **cucumber**, and two-inch long slices of **celery** for dipping.

• PINE NUT SPREAD

Some people call this "cheese spread." I prefer to make it without salt.

Soak:
One and a half cups **pine nuts** for one hour, or for up to a day, then drain water.

Combine in Cuisinart:
The soaked **pine nuts**
Juice of one **lemon**
Three tablespoons **nutritional yeast**
Two generous tablespoons **dill**
4 raw **walnuts**
One-half teaspoon **salt** (optional)
One teaspoon **pro-biotic powder** (optional)

Optional:
If you want it spicy, add a dash or two of **cayenne powder**, or **chili powder**.

This can be used as a spread on seed or veggie pulp **crackers**, or on sliced **carrots or celery**.

To make a **collard green burrito**: On a collard leaf, spread some of this pine cheese with **avocado, sprouts, walnuts**, and a dash of **salt** and/or dash of **dulse powder**. You might also add some of the Mexican Paté from the previous recipe.

• MARINARA

In the morning, put three-fourths cup of chopped **sundried tomatoes** in water, and let them soak all day.

Combine in food processor until still slightly chunky:
The soaked **sundried tomatoes** (with water strained out)
Three cups chopped **tomatoes**
One-half **red bell pepper**
One clove minced fresh **garlic**
One-fourth cup chopped fresh **basil**, or one tablespoon dried
One small palm full of chopped fresh **oregano**, or one teaspoon dried
Two or three pinches **black pepper**
One or two pinches **cayenne powder** (or more, depending on if you like spicy)
One-fourth teaspoon of either **salt or dulse powder**, depending on your taste. Or a little of both.
Two to three tablespoons organic, cold-pressed **olive oil or hemp seed oil**.

Chill and serve over shredded **zucchini** (cut with a spiralizer) **or raw kelp noodles**

Note:
Because of the herb taste opening up, this marinara may taste better on the second day: keep in fridge.

Optional:

This is a marinara recipe you can experiment with to make a taste sensation that is most pleasant to you.

While it is blending add one or more of the following:

One or two pitted, diced **olives** as the sauce is blending
Three or four crumbled **walnuts**
Several **pine nuts** that have been soaked in water for one to ten hours One-fourth teaspoon **cumin**
One-fourth teaspoon **sage**
One-fourth teaspoon **dill**.
One teaspoon of freshly minced **ginger root**

When it is ladled over shredded zucchini, sprinkle some **nutritional yeast** and/or **sesame seeds** on top...
Unless, you don't use nutritional yeast.

• GRAVY

In a Cuisinart, combine:
One **burdock root**, chopped fine
One thumb-sized piece of a **brown onion**
One pitted **date**
Four tablespoons raw **tahini**
Three tablespoons either **olive, flax, or hemp oil**
A pinch of **dulse powder**
One-fourth teaspoon pink or sea **salt** (optional)
One-fourth teaspoon **black pepper**
A little **water** to make the gravy the consistency you desire

Optional:

One-third cup **dried shiitake mushroom powder**: made by putting shiitake mushroom in a coffee grinder or a high-speed blender.

Hummus

• Rocking Raw Hummus

It takes two to three days to germinate the garbanzo beans.

Note: the word being used is *germinate*, and not *sprouted*. You only want a small root on the garbanzos, and not to grow them into sprouts, which is the point at which they would have leaves.

If you are going to use garbanzo beans (you can also use three cups peeled zucchini):

Soak in water for several hours:
One-and-a-half cups dry, raw **garbanzo beans**
After soaking, strain the water out. Keep in covered bowl. Place in a colander and rinse two or three times per day. Keep in clean, covered bowl (it is good to change the bowl every time you rinse them. They are ready when the root tail is about one-fourth-inch long. This should create about three cups of germinated garbanzo beans.

Stir five slices of **sundried tomato** with olive oil (just enough to get them soaked), and let them sit in a covered bowl for a day.

Note: some people who are otherwise raw will steam the germinated garbanzo beans for ten minutes and let them cool down before they proceed with the rest of the recipe. This is because they feel that germinated garbanzo beans that have been steamed are easier to digest.

Combine all of the following in a Vitamix and blend it while tamping it down with the tamper to get everything really smoothly blended (A Cuisinart can also be used, but a Vitamix makes it more smooth).

About three cups **germinated garbanzo beans**

One-fourth cup **olive or hemp oil**

Fresh **lemon juice** from three lemons, or four small lemons

Five or six cloves **garlic**

Thumb-sized piece **brown onion**

One teaspoon **dulse powder**

One teaspoon pink or sea **salt** (optional)

Tomato, one-half of a fresh tomato

Several **sundried tomatoes** blend easier if dice them or cut them with kitchen scissors

Nine or ten **raw olives**

Nutritional yeast, about three heaping tablespoons

Black pepper, about one-half teaspoon

One-fourth teaspoon **cayenne powder**

One teaspoon **dill**

One teaspoon **paprika**

Basil, fresh, a generous palm full of leaves (or tablespoon dried)

Raw tahini, about three tablespoons

Red bell pepper, about one-fourth of a large red bell pepper cut into pieces

One teaspoon vegan **probiotic powder**

Serve with carrot slices, celery slices, broccoli slices, red bell slices, and apple slices.

Or make green burrito by spreading on kale or collard leaves with sprouts, shredded carrots, chopped cilantro, and slices of avocado. Then roll into a burrito.

You can use this hummus in the following recipe:

• NO BEAN HUMMUS

By Matt Amsden of RawVolution.
Access: rawvolution.com

In high-speed blender, combine until thick and smooth:
Two **zucchini**, peeled and chopped
Three-fourths cup raw **tahini**
One-half cup fresh **lemon juice**
One-fourth cup **olive oil**
Four cloves **garlic**, peeled
Two and a half teaspoons **sea salt** (optional)
One half tablespoon ground **cumin**

Chill.

You can use this hummus in the following recipe:

• XAM'S HUMMUS

In Cuisinart, grind together:
One and a half cups **sunflower seeds**
One and a half cups **cashews**

Put ground sunflower seeds/cashew mix into high-

speed blender, and add:
Two tablespoons **tamari** (Ohsawa brand organic unpasteurized wheat-free tamari)
One tablespoon **turmeric root powder**
One teaspoon **cayenne**
Two tablespoons **nutritional yeast** (optional)
One teaspoon **tarragon**
One teaspoon **cumin seeds**
One crushed clove of **garlic**
One tablespoon cold pressed **olive oil**
About one cup **water** (and maybe a little more while blending).

Blend until consistency is smooth.

Top falafels with hummus. Serve on plate with side of more hummus along with slices of **cucumbers** and **carrots** and a salad.

WRAPS

You can take just about any salad, chop it up, and use it as a filler in a wrap. You can also use raw hummus, raw pate, guacamole, raw vegan taco filler, nut cheeses, sprouts, and even apples, mango, and other fruit in combination with a variety of shredded vegetables.

Raw fooders often use collard greens to make wraps. Some dip the collard in hot water to soften it, but others say that is damaging some of the nutrients.

Some people use cabbage leaves, romaine or butter lettuce leaves, broccoli leaves as wraps.

If someone is vegan fusion (they eat both cooked and raw vegan foods), they may use a corn or sprouted grain tortilla.

Raw tortillas can be made out of a variety of ingredients, such as the raw tortilla chip recipes in this book. To keep the tortilla sort, simply don't dehydrate it all the way, keeping it soft and pliable.

Ingredient Ideas for Wraps:

Choose a variety of fillings of various colors, textures, and flavors. Mix and match until you find your favorite wrap filler.

Dressing:
Guacamole
Hummus

Pâté
Salad dressing
Nut cheeses

Herbs, spices, and flavorings:
Cayenne
Coriander
Black pepper
Turmeric
Paprika
Dill
Cumin
Lime juice
Lemon juice
Dulse flakes
Kelp powder
Onion powder
Sage

Leafy greens, chopped fine:
Italian parsley
Basil
Chard
Kale
Spinach
Cilantro
Purslane
Dandelion
Green onions
Broccoli leaf
Oregano
Cabbage

Sprouts:
Broccoli sprouts

Sunflower sprouts
Alfalfa sprouts
Clover sprouts

Vegetables, sliced long, shredded, or diced:
Carrots
Celery
Red, yellow, or orange bell pepper (actually a fruit)
Red, white, or brown onion
Broccoli
Cauliflower
Jicama
Mushrooms (actually, a fungi, not a vegetable)

Fruit, sliced, cubed, or diced:
Tomatoes
Cucumbers
Zucchini
Grapes or raisins
Apples
Pears
Asian pear
Peaches
Mango
Currants
Goji berries
Dates
Green olives

Nuts, fractured:
Walnuts
Macadamia nuts
Almonds
Pecans
Cashews (which are actually a fruit, not a nut)

Seeds:
Hemp seeds
Sunflower seeds
Millet

• MUSHROOM WRAP FILLER

Combine in Cuisinart:
One portabella **mushroom**, chopped
One **carrot**
Five **walnuts**
One-fourth of a **brown onion**, chopped
Five raw, pitted **green olives**
One tablespoon **hemp oil**
One tablespoon **thyme**
Dash of **cayenne powder**
One half teaspoon pink or sea **salt** (optional)

After combining the above ingredients in Cuisinart, place in bowl and stir in finely cubed **avocado**.

Use as filler for a **collard green** wrap by putting a scoop full on a collard leaf and wrapping it up.

SIDES

• AMERICAN WILD RICE PILAF

First day:
Soak in water overnight:
Two cups organic **wild rice**

Second day:
Pour the soaking wild rice into screen mesh colander to drain out the water, and rinse with more water for several seconds.
Pour the rice into a clean bowl, cover with a plate, and keep at room temperature for 24 hours.

Third day:
The rice has become soft, many of the grains have split open, and the rice is ready to use. Put this germinated rice in a large bowl.

Dice well and toss in bowl with the rice:
Two ribs of **celery**
One-half of a **cucumber**
One large or two smaller **carrots**
Two **green onions**
One **avocado**, peeled and pitted (avocado is optional)
A fist-full of **Italian parsley**
One-fourth of a **red onion**

Stir in:
Juice of one-half **lemon**
Two tablespoons **olive or hemp seed oil**

Cut in halves or fourths:
Several small **tomatoes,** such as grape tomatoes, and scatter on top of rest of ingredients as a garnish.

Optional:
One-fourth cup **black currants, black pepper, dill weed**, a dash of **paprika** to garnish.

• PRESSED RED CABBAGE CARAWAY SLAW

By Nomi Shannon, author of *The Raw Gourmet*; RawGourmet.com

Makes four to six servings.

Six cups thinly sliced **red cabbage** (about one-half of a large cabbage)
One large white **onion**, sliced thin
One teaspoon sea **salt** (optional)
One tablespoon **caraway seeds**
Two teaspoons **coconut aminos**

Place vegetables in bowl. Sprinkle the sea salt, caraway seeds and liquid aminos evenly over vegetables. With your hands, knead and toss the salad, crushing the vegetables in your hands for five to six minutes. Chill and serve.

• Sea Vegetable Slaw

Soak in water:
One handful **dulse** or **hijiki** seaweed, chopped

Chop and toss in bowl:
Four cups of shredded red or green **cabbage**
One bunch of **cilantro**
One half cup chopped **scallions**
Dashes of **seasoning** of your choice: black pepper,
thyme, dill, or other vegetable seasoning.

Optional:
Thin slices of **red or white onion**. Diced **red bell
pepper**. Dashes of **hemp seed or flax oil, salt, vinega**r.

Drain:
Water from the seaweed.

Mix all ingredients, massaging the ingredients together
with your hands. Chill, and serve.

• Marinated Mushrooms

This recipe can be made a day in advance.

In a bowl, mix together
One-fourth cup **hemp seed oil or olive oil**
One tablespoon Ohsawa brand organic unpasteurized
wheat-free **tamari**
The juice from one half of a **lemon**
One-fourth cup minced Italian **parsley**
One minced **green onion**

One or two minced **garlic** cloves
One-half teaspoon **salt** (optional)
One pinch **white pepper** powder
One pinch **kelp** powder

Using a spoon, scrape out the gills of:
Six **portobello mushrooms** with stems removed
Then cut each mushroom cap in half and thinly slice.

Put the slices of mushroom in the bowl of the marinara mixture. Mix so the mushroom slices are coated. Allow to marinate at room temperature for one to two hours. Then, cover and keep refrigerated.

Serve at room temperature.

These can be served inside a kale leave along with guacamole and wrapped. Also good with caulirice recipe below.

• CAULIRICE

One half a head of a **cauliflower** (cut into bits)
One **tomato** (cut into fourths)
One half **red bell pepper** (cut into bits)
One cup fresh **parsley** (cut up)
One forth cup fresh **chives**

Place in food processor and process until the texture of couscous or brown rice. Can be served with grave and burger recipe above. Or wrap a scoop full in a Romaine lettuce with slices of tomato and avocado.

Optional:
One or more of the following can be added: crumbled palm-full of raw **walnuts**; one tablespoon of **chili powder**; **currants**; diced **olives**: one-fourth cup diced **red onion**; tablespoon of raw **hemp seed oil** or palm full of fractured raw **hemp seeds**.

• MASHED NOT POTATOES

Soak in water for half an hour:
One a half cup **cashews**

Rinse the cashews.

Drain the cashews, and combine in a high-speed blender with:
One chopped **cauliflower**
One-fourth cup chopped **parsnips**
Two tablespoons **flaxseed or olive oil**
Juice of one **lemon**
One-fourth teaspoon **salt** (optional)

Use the blender tamper to keep tamping down the mixture until it is smooth.

If you don't have a high-speed blender, the ingredients can be put through a Champion juicer using the blank plate, then further blended in a standard kitchen blender or in a food processor until smooth.

Pour into serving bowl. Garnish with diced Italian parsley. Serve at room temperature, or chill.

Optional:
These may also be blended in:
One **crimini mushroom**
One thumb-sized slice of **brown onion**

• HEMP SEED TABOULI

In a large bowl, stir together:
Three bunches **Italian parsley**, finely chopped
One-third cup **hemp seeds**
Several **cherry or grape tomatoes** cut n half
One-fourth cup **brown onion**, finely chopped
Two or three tablespoons **hemp seed oil**
Juice of one **lemon**
One-fourth teaspoon pink or sea **salt** (optional)

Optional:
One teaspoon **dill**. One tablespoon unheated, raw
millet. Diced **red bell pepper**.

Chill.

• MEGAN ELIZABETH'S FALAFELS
To find more of Megan's recipes, access:
MeganElizabeth.com

Soak in water overnight or up to a day:
Three-fourths cup hulled, raw **sunflower seeds**

Rinse the seeds in a colander, then spread on a towel to
let dry for half a day

In a food processor, combine:
The **sunflower seeds** with:
Two cups chopped **carrots**
One-half to one cup chopped **cilantro**
One-half cup chopped **green onions**
One teaspoon **lime juice**
One-half teaspoon **coriander seeds**
One-half teaspoon **cumin seeds**

You may need to use a spatula to

Form into balls and roll in:
Sesame seeds

Chill in the refrigerator for about half and hour to help them firm up.

While they can be kept in the fridge for a few days, the falafel balls seem to use their flavor, and are best eaten on the day you make them.

Tahini dressing:
One-half tablespoon **sesame tahini**
Tablespoon of **water**
Tablespoon of **veggie juice**

Place the falafel in leaves of **red cabbage** with:
Butter or romaine lettuce
Chopped **tomatoes**
Chopped **cilantro**
Drizzle of **tahini sauce**

• RAW CURRY FALAFEL

From Xam Devesh of the Xammin' UnBakery.
Xammin.blogspot.com

In large bowl, stir together:
One and a half cups **flax seeds**
One and a half cups **sunflower seeds**
One and a half tablespoon **turmeric root powder**
One teaspoon whole **cumin seeds**
Two teaspoons **paprika**
One tablespoon **red pepper flakes**
One teaspoon **cayenne powder**
Two teaspoons **tarragon leaves**
Two teaspoons ground **mustard seed**

Then add wet ingredients, and stir all together:
Two tablespoons **tamari** (Oshawa brand organic
unpasteurized wheat-free tamari)
Two tablespoons cold-pressed **olive oil**
One-half cup **water**

Pat into six falafels. Place on **dehydrator** trays.
Dehydrate for three hours about 105 degrees F. Then
flip, and dehydrate another three hours.

BURGERS, LOAFS, TACO FILLER, AND STUFFED BELL

• SUNFOOD BURGERS

In a coffee grinder, grind together:
One cup raw, dehulled **sunflower seeds** (may have to do one-half cup first)
and a sprinkle of raw **pumpkin seeds**

Chop fine:
One **Roma tomato**, or other medium tomato
One handful of **broccoli**
One brown **onion**
Optional:
A palm full of chopped **red bell pepper** and/or **crimini mushrooms**

Blend until the consistency of breadcrumbs:
One-palm full of **walnuts or Brazil nuts**

Shred:
One **carrot**
Two **zucchini**

Stir the above together with:
One tablespoon **cumin**
One teaspoon **coriander**

One teaspoon **thyme**
One teaspoon **turmeric**
One-half teaspoon **wakame or dulse seaweed powder**

Optional:
You might also add a little **pink salt, cayenne pepper** [if you like hot spice], and **black pepper.**

Make palm-sized burgers. Place in dehydrator for 8 to 15 hours (depending on how firm you like the burgers).

While the burgers are dehydrating, make the topping.

Topping: in a small processor, blend all of these together:
One cup **pine nuts**
Three tablespoons **nutritional yeast**
One-half teaspoon **dill**
The juice from one half of a **lemon**
One-fourth teaspoon **pink salt** or a combination of salt and **dulse powder.**

Chill the topping.

When the burgers are ready, spread the topping on top, and add a slice of **tomato**, some diced **avocado**, and wrap in a **collard green** with some **sprouts.**

Collard greens: Some people like to soften them by heating some water, then pouring the hot water over the collard green as it sits in a bowl. I prefer my collards full strength.

Nice to serve these with a salad.

• VEGGIE NUT LOAF (OR BURGERS)

Soak in water for several hours or overnight:
One cup raw **almonds**
Two cups raw **sunflower seeds**
One-fourth cup **sesame seeds**

Strain:
The water out of the almonds, sunflower seeds, and
sesame seeds after they are done soaking.

In food processor, combine until rough:
All of the almonds, sunflower seeds, and sesame seeds.

Grate:
Enough carrots to make one-half cup **shredded carrots**

Chop:
Parsley to equal one-half cup
Shallots to equal one-half cup
Dulse to equal one-fourth cup, or use slightly less dulse
powder

Grind roughly in coffee grinder:
One-half cup raw, dehulled **pumpkin seeds**

Optional, one or more of the following:
Tablespoon of **thyme**. Two minced cloves of **garlic**.
Teaspoon ground **black pepper**. One-fourth cup diced
brown onion. Several diced small raw **mushrooms**. A
few tablespoons raw **millet**.

Place:
All of the ingredients in a big bowl and use a big spoon
or your hands to mix everything together.

Either form into a loaf, such as by putting into a glass
loaf pan. Or make into patties. If desired, the patties can
be dehydrated until more firm. Otherwise, the loaf or
burgers can be served right away.

• VEGGIE LOAF WITH GRAVY

Soak:
Three-fourths cup dehulled raw **sunflower seeds**
Three-fourths cup raw **walnuts**
Three-fourths cup raw **Brazil nuts or almonds**

Lightly grind in coffee grinder:
One fresh sprig, or one teaspoon dried **rosemary**
One tablespoon **thyme**
One teaspoon **sage**

**Combine in Cuisinart the following into a crumb-
like consistency:**
The nuts and herb mix with:
One-fourth cup **olive oil or hemp oil**
One-half teaspoon **dulse powder**
One teaspoon pink or sea **salt** (optional)
One-half teaspoon **black pepper**

Mince:
Two ribs of **celery**
One half **red bell pepper**
One fistful **Italian parsley**

One-half inch **ginger root**
Three cloves of **garlic**
Four **crimini mushrooms** (optional)

In a large bowl, hand mix together:
The nut/herb combination with the minced vegetables.

Form into two loafs on a platter. Serve chilled, OR place in dehydrator at 118 degrees for ten to fifteen hours.

Can also be served with gravy recipe.

• STUFFED RED BELL PEPPERS
From Anand Wells and Runi Burton of Australia's
LiveFoodEducation.com

Soak in salty water for eight hours:
Four cups **pecans**

Soak in water for two hours:
One cup **sundried tomatoes**

Put in a food processor and pulse until consistency is not too smooth, but not too lumpy:
The two cups of soaked **pecans**
The one cup of dried **tomatoes**
One medium **carrot**, chopped into small pieces for easy processing
One medium **zucchini**, chopped into small pieces for easy processing
Two **dates**, pitted
One-half teaspoon Celtic **salt** (optional)
Two tablespoons **chia seeds**

One tablespoon **lemon juice**
One clove of **garlic**

Optional:
One **chili**

Slice in half (either through the middle or top to bottom) and scrape out the seeds:
Six red bell peppers (in Australia they are called *capsicums*)
Fill the bell peppers with the mixture from the food processor. You can eat them straight away or dehydrate them at 115 degrees Fahrenheit for four hours.

Serves six.

FIESTA

• TACO FILLER

This taco filler can be used in taco salad, or as filler in raw vegan tacos made using romaine lettuce leaves as shells.

Soak in water for several hours:
Two cups **walnuts**

Drain the walnuts, spread on a dry towel to absorb access water.

Put the walnuts in food processor.

Pulse a little at a time until crumbly, but not fine. You don't want them to turn into nut butter.

Add the rest of ingredients to food processor and pulse until desired consistency:
One-fourth cup chopped **sundried tomatoes**
Two tablespoons minced **brown onion**
Two to three tablespoons **chili powder**
One tablespoon **cumin**
One tablespoon dried **oregano** or three or four tablespoons minced fresh oregano
A pinch **cayenne**

Optional:
Salt to taste.
One-half teaspoon **dulse flakes**
One teaspoon **celery powder**
One teaspoon **red bell pepper powder**
One tablespoon **lime juice**
One teaspoon minced **jalapeno**
One teaspoon **carob powder**

Onion powder can be used if a fresh onion isn't available.

• Dehydrating onions, celery, and red bell pepper

If you have a dehydrator, you can make dehydrated onion powder. Simply dice a few brown onions. Spread the diced onion on a solid dehydrator sheet.

Dehydrate at about 110 to 115 degrees for 3 to 6 hours.

Then scrape off onto the mesh sheet, spreading the onion around evenly, and dehydrate another 4 to 8 hours – or until very dry.

Place in a blender or food processor and blend until powder. Keep in a glass jar I the refrigerator for use in recipes.

The same can be done with celery and red bell pepper.

Celery powder can taste a bit salty to people who don't use salt, and is a good substitute to use instead of salt for those avoiding the use of salt.

• TACO SALAD INGREDIENT IDEAS

Taco filler from above recipe
Chopped **romaine or iceberg lettuce**
Diced **cilantro**
Diced **avocado**
Diced **red onion**
Diced **tomato**
Shredded **carrot**
Chopped **green olives**
Spiced and dehydrated sprouted **pumpkin seeds***

* Spiced dehydrated pumpkin seeds

This recipe can doubled, tripled, or quadrupled and the well-dried spiced seeds stored in glass container in a cool, dry place for up to a couple of months.

This can also be done using sunflower seeds.

Soak in water for a few hours:
One-half cup of raw, hulled **pumpkin seeds**

Strain the water.

Put wet pumpkin seeds in bowl, add:
One tablespoon **chili powder**
One or two tablespoons diced **brown onion**
One tablespoon minced **jalapeno**
One tablespoon **cumin** powder
One big pinch of **cayenne powder**
One tablespoon **dulse flakes**
One or two tablespoons **lime juice**

Mix with spoon until all pumpkin seeds are mixed well with the other ingredients.

Let it sit in the bowl for about a half hour.

Spread evenly on solid dehydrator sheet.

Dehydrate at 110-115 degrees, for 4 to 8 hours, or until very dry. Store in a cool place in a glass jar.

• PICO DE GALLO

Two or three large **tomatoes** with seed bed removed, then diced
One-fourth cup diced **cilantro**
One small **red onion**, diced. About one-third cup.
One **jalapeno**, seeded and minced
One or two tablespoons **lime or lemon juice**

Optional:
Salt to taste

• SOUR CREAM

Soak for 1 to 3 hours:
One cup **cashews**

Drain the water.

Put the soaked cashews in high-speed blender, and combine with:

Two tablespoons **lemon juice**
One teaspoon **apple cider vinegar**
One-quarter cup of **water**, than add additional water by the tablespoon as blending until desired consistency is reached
One big pinch of **salt**

Optional:
One teaspoon **vegan probiotic powder**

• RAW UNFRIED NONBEANS

Soak in water for four to eight hours:

In one bowl, place:
One-third cup chopped **sundried tomatoes**
Cover with water

In second bowl, place:
Two cups raw, hulled **sunflower seeds**
Cover with water

After four to eight hours:

Keep the water from the sundried tomatoes.

Toss the water from the sunflower seeds.

In food processor using an S blade or in a high-speed blender, combine:
The **tomatoes** and **sunflower** seeds

Use some of the **water from soaking the tomatoes,** adding it only by the tablespoon until the desired smooth tomato paste consistency is reached

Add these ingredients and blend until smooth:
One-half cup chopped **cilantro**
One or two cloves **garlic**, crushed and minced
One-half **jalapeno**, deseeded and then diced
Two tablespoons diced **green onion**
One teaspoon **lemon juice**
One-half teaspoon **cumin** powder
One-half teaspoon **chili powder**

Optional oil choices:
If you don't use bottled oils, and you are going to use this recipe within several hours, you can use half an **avocado**.

Or, if you are a person who uses bottled oils, you can use one-fourth cup cold pressed organic **olive oil.**

If you don't want to use either, you can use **water**, added by the tablespoon while blending only until the desired consistency is reached. The sunflower seeds do contain some natural oil.

• RAW CORN CHIPS OR SHELLS

In a high-speed blender, combine:
Four cups of organic fresh or frozen **corn**
One-quarter cup of diced **yellow or orange bell pepper**
One or two cloves of **garlic**, minced
One teaspoon **turmeric**
One teaspoon **cumin**
Three or four tablespoons **lime juice**

One cup of **water**, and a little more, added a little at a time until mixture is combined well

Pour in the mixture from the blender into a bowl containing:
Two cups freshly ground **golden flax seed**

Options:
Two tablespoons **olive, hemp, or coconut oil** –
depending on your taste preferences
One quarter **avocado**
One quarter cup raw **hemp seeds**
One quarter cup soaked **almonds**

Other options:
One-quarter **brown onion**, diced
Two tablespoons **chili powder**
Two tablespoons **nutritional yeast**
A few tablespoons diced **cilantro**
One and a half teaspoons **paprika**
A few pinches of **black pepper**

Salt options:
If you use salt, you can either put it in the mixture, or you can sprinkle it on the mixture after you spread the corn mixture on the dehydrator sheet.

Place the Teflex or other solid dehydrator sheet directly on the counter.

Spread the corn mix thinly on the dehydrator sheet. Use an offset/long metal spatula, dipping it into water to make it easier to spread. (You can also spread only the size of a taco shell to make rounds that can be used for toppings.)

Once the mixture is spread on the sheet, dehydrate at 110 to 115 degrees for a few hours then remove and use a knife to score them in either a criss-cross pattern for chips, or in squares that can be used for topping to serves as canapés or antojitos.

Place the trays back into the dehydrator and dehydrate for an additional few hours. Remove and place a mesh dehydrator sheet and then a tray on top of them. Flip the trays over, removing the top tray and the solid dehydrator sheet.

Place back into the dehydrator for a few more hours, until crisp.

• RAW CHIA FRESCA FOR FOUR

In a blender, blend until dates are obliterated:
One-half cup **lime juice**
Four tablespoons **chia seeds**
Two pitted **dates**
Big pinch of **cinnamon**
Four cups **water**

Optional:
One pinch of **salt**
Instead of dates, use four tablespoons **maple syrup**
Instead of water, use fresh **coconut water**
You can also mince a one-forth inch piece of **fresh ginger root**, and blend that in with the other ingredients

After blending, thinly slice **strawberries**, and let them float in the fresca

Chill for an hour or so.

• RAW VEGAN FLAN

Yes, flan is traditionally made of eggs, milk, and sugar. But, it can also be made the raw vegan way. While there are vegan recipes for chocolate flan, berry flan, even pumpkin flan, this recipe aims to be more in alignment with the traditional flan, but in a vegan way.

No cow farm, egg farm, or processed sugar is needed here.

Soak in water for an hour or two:
Four pitted **dates**

In a blender, blend until coconut is smooth and dates are obliterated:
Two cups **young coconut meat**
One-fourth cup **chia seeds**
Two tablespoons **powdered agar agar**
One tablespoon **vanilla**

Optional:
One teaspoon minced or grated **orange rind** (shavings of an orange peel)
Half a cup of soaked **cashews**

After blending to a satisfactory consistency, pour into four flan molds on a flat desert plate, or in remenkin dishes or teacups. Refrigerate from an hour, or up to a day.

When ready to serve, if using the flan mold, simply remove the mold, and drizzle with date/yacon mix below.

If using the remekin dishes, simply leave the flan in the dish and drizzle with the date/yacon mix.

If using the teacups, leave in the cup. Or gently slip a knife around the edges, separating the flan from the sides of the cup, then flip upside down on small plate. If flan doesn't slip from the cup onto the plate, run hot water over the teacup while it is upside down on the plate. The flan should drop onto the plate and you can remove the cup. Be sure to not let the flan fall from the plate when you tip it to let the water drip off.

You can decorate with berries, edible flowers, a slice of lime, and/or drizzle with the following:

Drizzle for top of flan:
In blender or food processor, combine:
Four pitted and soaked **dates**
One tablespoon **yacon root syrup**
Teaspoon **vanilla**
A squeeze of **lemon or lime juice**

Optional:
Tablespoon or two of **maple syrup**
Tablespoon **coconut sugar crystals**
Pinch or two of **salt**

PÂTÉ

• CABBAGE PUMPKIN SEED PÂTÉ

Soak for 2 hours, and then drain:
One cup **pumpkin seeds**

In food processor, mix the pumpkin seeds with all of the following:
One-fourth chopped head of **cabbage**
One-half cup **water**
One tablespoon **herbs de province**
One teaspoon **marjoram**
One-half teaspoon **cumin**
One-half teaspoon **paprika**
One stalk fresh **rosemary** (or 1 tablespoon dried)
One-half teaspoon **lemon thyme**
One-eighth teaspoon **cayenne**
Pinch of **sea salt**
Place all ingredients in food processor with s-blade attached. Process until smooth. Serve with **flax crackers** and/or **cucumber sticks**.

• VEGETABLE PÂTÉ

One-third cup **pumpkin seeds**
Seven **walnuts**
One small **zucchini**, chopped

One-fourth cup **brown onion,** chopped
One-third of a **red bell pepper,** chopped
Juice of one **lemon**
Two or three **garlic** cloves
Two tablespoons **dulse powder**
One tablespoon **kelp powder**
Three to four tablespoons **nutritional yeast**
Cherry-sized piece of **ginger root,** diced
One medium **carrot,** chopped
One-fourth teaspoon **black pepper**
Dash of **dark or apple vinegar**

Combine all ingredients in Cuisinart. Use as spread on
dehydrated veggie pulp or seed crackers.

Optional:
Some people use two tablespoons of Nama Shoyu in this
recipe. I don't.

• MEXICAN PÂTÉ

Combine all in a Cuisinart:
Juice from half a **lemon**
One-fourth cup freshly ground (in coffee grinder)
pumpkin seeds
One-fourth cup freshly ground (in coffee grinder) **flax
seeds**
One **carrot,** chopped
One-fourth **tomato**
One-fourth of a **green pepper,** chopped
Three cloves **garlic,** crushed and diced
6 raw **walnuts**
6 raw **Brazil nuts** (or 6 more walnuts)

Two tablespoons **hemp oil**
One-fourth teaspoon **black pepper**
One-half teaspoon **salt** (optional)
Four tablespoons **cumin**
Two tablespoons **chili pepper powder**

Serve chilled.

For rawduerves, serve on slices of **tomato** or raw **seed crackers**. Top with **avocado** and a bit of **sprouts**.

Optional: If you like cilantro, instead of using a carrot, use an entire bunch of **cilantro**, including the stems. You might also add four pitted green **olives**, a dash of **vinegar**, and a small piece of a **carrot**.

• INDIAN PÂTÉ

Combine all in a Cuisinart:
One cup raw **walnuts**
One quarter cup chopped **dried tomatoes**
One cup chopped **celery**
One cup chopped **carrots**
Half teaspoon **curry** powder
Quarter teaspoon of **cumin**
Half teaspoon **hempseed oil**

Optional:
Palm full of chopped **green onions**
Diced clove of **garlic**
One quarter cup fresh or frozen **organic peas**
Salt or dulse flakes

Use as a wrap made of a red cabbage or collard leaf with:

Chopped **tomatoes**

Chopped **cilantro or Italian parsley**

Chopped and marinated **mushrooms** that have been marinated in a mixture of

One teaspoon of **chickpea miso**

One diced clove of **garlic**

One teaspoon of **hempseed oil**

Two or three tablespoons of **water**

CHIPS AND CRACKERS

• ZUCCHINI CHIPS

Slice **zucchini** thinly. Place in a dehydrator set to about
105 degrees until dry. Use with dips, pâté, and
guacamole.

The same can be done with **carrots, summer squash,
pears**, and **apples**.

• HEMP CORN CHIPS
Needed: a dehydrator to dry the dough into crackers.

Soak in water for one to three hours:
Six cups **sunflower seeds**

Grind in a coffee grinder until grainy powder:
2 cups raw **flax seeds**

In a food processor, combine until creamy:
Six cups fresh **corn** cut off the cob
One cup (or a more, if needed) **water**

Strain and rinse the sunflower seeds

In food processor, combine until creamy:
The sunflower seeds

With enough water to make the mixture creamy

Stir together in large bowl:
The creamed corn
The creamed sunflower seeds
One cup fractured **hemp seeds**
One-fourth cup **cumin powder**
One tablespoon **cayenne powder** (optional)
One-tablespoon sea **salt or dulse** powder (optional)
Juice of one **lime**

Spread on dehydrator sheets:
The mixture, about one-fourth- to one-third-inch thick.
Place in dehydrator at 105 degrees for twenty to twenty-four hours. After about five or six hours, use a dull knife to score triangular criss-cross lines into the dough so that, when they are done the next day, the dried dough will break into the size of crackers you wish to have. After about ten hours, gently flip over. They should be crispy dry when done. They should easily break apart along the score lines.

• DEHYDRATED CRACKERS

If you have been around raw food enough, you have likely seen a variety of dehydrated, non-baked crackers. It seems there are as many recipes for raw dehydrated crackers as there are people that make them.

Step one:
If you have a Champion Juicer, you can take the pulp left over from making half a gallon of vegetable juice, and, using your hands, combine the veggie pulp two cups of

flax seeds, a cup of raw pumpkin seeds, a cup of dill, and then let this sit for an hour. If you have to go out, put this in the fridge for up to a day.

Step two - optional:
Take the mixture of pulp/flax/pumpkin/dill, and, if you use oil or salt, use your hands to mix in up to half a cop of raw olive oil and up to two tablespoons of pink or sea salt. You may also add a tablespoon of dulse powder.

Step three:
Spread the mixture approximately one-fourth-inch thick on the dehydrator sheets. Dehydrate them at about 105 to 110 degrees for 8 or more hours. How long they take to dry into crackers will be determined by the humidity in the atmosphere, the temperature of the room, and the moisture in the pulp. It may take 8 hours, or it may take 20 hours. As you get used to making crackers, you will be able to determine how long it will take to dry them.

Simple flax seed crackers:
Another version of raw, dehydrated crackers may also only contain three ingredients: Five cups of flax seeds that have been soaked in water for a few hours and drained, and then mixed with a cup of dill weed, a tablespoon of dulse powder and/or salt, and a dash of cayenne pepper. Spread out thinly (about one-fourth-inch thick) on dehydrator sheets and dehydrate at about 105 to 110 degrees for about 7 to 10 hours.

Simple flax seed crackers, 2nd recipe:
Another recipe for crackers involves combining four carrots in a food processor with one teaspoon salt, one-half teaspoon black pepper, and a dash of cayenne. Then putting this mixture in a bowl and stirring in 3 cups of

soaked flax seeds. Spread out about one-fourth-inch thick on dehydrator sheets and dehydrate at about 105 to 110 degrees for 8 to 20 hours. An option with this is to add the flax in with the carrots, black pepper, and dash of cayenne, and also blend in one cup of firmly packed spinach. When you dry this on a dehydrator, it will be more like green tortilla chips, especially if you increase the cayenne, and maybe add a tablespoon of cumin.

Look at various raw recipe books and see what ingredients they have in their crackers. You will get your own ideas, and develop your own cracker recipes. Or, like me, you may never pay attention to cracker recipes, and make them different almost every time.

SOUPS

• TOMATO SOUP

In high-speed blender, combine:
Three cups **tomatoes**
Two or three stalks **celery**
One-half of a peeled **lemon**
One minced clove of **garlic**
One-half bunch of chopped **cilantro**

Chill and serve in bowls. Sprinkle with diced fresh **cilantro** or **dill** leaf. This could go well with some of the crackers in the following recipe, such as dill/flax crackers.

Optional:
If you like your soup sweet, have it as it is. For a spicier soup, while it is blending, add half a diced fresh **hot pepper**. You can also add some **chili powder**. If you don't stay away from salt, add some pinches of **salt**, or powdered **dulse**.

• CARROT SOUP

Juice:
Enough **carrots** to make one-and-a-half-cups juice
Keep about one cup of the carrot pulp

Juice:

Enough **celery** to make one-and-a-half-cups juice

Dice:

A palm full of fresh **dill** (or use one tablespoon dried dill)

Two **Romaine tomatoes**, or enough of your favorite tomatoes to make a cup of diced tomatoes

One-fourth of a **red bell pepper**

Three inches of a **cucumber**

The flesh of one ripe **avocado**

In a blender, combine:

The carrot juice, celery juice, dill, and avocado.

Pour:

The blender mixture into a large bowl.

Stir in:

The tomatoes, bell pepper, cucumber, and carrot pulp.

Serve chilled. Garnish with a dash of sesame seeds and/or millet.

Optional:

One-half teaspoon **dulse powder**. Blend in with the liquids.

• CATCH A HEALTHY HABIT SPINACH SOUP

By Glen Colello and Lisa Storch of Catch A Healthy Habit restaurant in
Fairfield, Connecticut; CatchAHealthyHabit.com

Serves three or four.

In a high-speed blender, combine:
One cup fresh **spinach**
One-half to one whole **cucumber** depending on the size
One to two **tomatoes** depending on the size
One-fourth cup pure "flouride free" **water**
One **avocado**, peeled and pitted
Two tablespoons **coconut aminos**
Pinch of **cayenne pepper**
One tablespoon fresh **lemon juice**
One tablespoon cold-pressed, raw olive oil

Chill and enjoy.

• PUMPKIN SOUP

From Maya Melamed of Taste Organic raw café in
Sydney, Australia. ChangingMaya.com.au.

In a high-speed blender, combine:
Two cups fresh cubed **kabocha pumpkin**
One-half cup of warm **water**
One cup **water of young Thai coconut**
One-fourth cup **flesh of young Thai coconut**
Three tablespoons of chopped fresh **cilantro** (leaves
only)
One-fourth teaspoon dried **ginger**
Cayenne pepper to taste

After blending:
Pour into bowls and sprinkle with **cinnamon**.

Optional:
Sea salt to taste.

• CHILLED TOMATO SOUP WITH AVOCADO SALSA FOR TWO

From Helen Castillo of TheRawPalate.com

With garden-fresh tomatoes in season, this quick and easy-to-make chilled soup with only five main ingredients is as comforting as Mom's, but made robust and lively with its garnish of avocado salsa that packs a punch of flavor in this savory dish.

In food processor, pulse the following until a puree:
Six large, juicy **tomatoes**, stemmed, seeded and cut into large chunks
Three Tablespoons **olive oil**
Two Tablespoons **shallot**, finely diced
Three Tablespoons fresh **lime juice**
Three-fourths teaspoon **Celtic sea salt** (optional)

In a serving bowl, toss until well combined:
One-half ripe, firm **Haas avocado**, peeled, pitted and diced
Two teaspoons finely diced **shallot**
Two teaspoons chopped fresh **cilantro**
Two teaspoons **olive oil**
Two Tablespoons fresh **lime juice**
Himalayan salt to taste (optional)

Transfer the soup from the food processor to salad bowls. Top with garnish.

• CREAM OF BROCCOLI SOUP

From Theresa Webb of Kitchen Buddy in England.
Theresa (at) KitchenBuddy.eu.

This is a great way to use fresh broccoli and is often liked by those who
don't like cooked broccoli.

In a high-speed blender, combine until a milk-like quality:
One handful **hemp seeds**
One cup **water**

Add in, and blend until smooth:
Two cups chopped broccoli
One cup chopped **cucumber**
One cup of chopped **celery** or **fennel**

Add in, and blend until fully combined:
One peeled and pitted **avocado**
Two teaspoons ground **flax seeds** (ground in a coffee grinder)

Optional:
Seaweed powder, such as **dulse**, to taste.
One half a chopped **bell pepper**, or one **tomato**,
blended in with other ingredients. The tomato or bell
pepper may also be diced, and then sprinkled on top of
soup as it is in the bowl, as a garnish.

For a thinner soup, add extra water, or for a thicker soup, add extra
avocado.

Optional recipe:

This soup can also be used to make **cabbage** or **spinach** soup, instead of broccoli.

Some cabbage or spinach can also be added to the broccoli soup as it is being blended.

Desserts

• Carrot Cake

Soak for one to three hours:
One cup **raw almonds** and three-fourths cup **dates** in water. Then drain water out and rinse in colander and let water drip out.

Juice:
Enough **carrots** to have one cup of pulp.
Save the juice for the recipe

In food processor, combine until formed into a ball:
The **almonds** that have been soaked
The **dates** that have been soaked

In large bowl, stir together:
The **carrot pulp**
Three-fourths cup **carrot juice**
The **almond/date** mixture
One-half cup **raisins**
One-fourth cup **shredded coconut**
One-half cup fractured **walnuts**
One tablespoon **ginger** powder
One teaspoon **cinnamon**
One-half teaspoon **nutmeg**
One tablespoon **lemon juice**
One tablespoon **orange zest** (orange peel)

After stirring the ingredients together (using your hands probably works best to mix the ingredients), shape into large ball, place on serving plate and form into a shape of a carrot cake.

Chill. Before serving, you can garnish it:

Garnish, optional, one or more of the following:
Sprinkle with **grated carrot**, **shredded coconut**, slices of **pineapple**, **berries** of your choice, or **edible flowers**

• CARROT CAKE ICING

Soak in water for one to three hours in water:
Four **dates**
Half cup of raw **cashews**
Then, drain the water

Juice:
One **orange**
Save part of the orange peel

In high-speed blender or food processor, combine until creamy smooth:
The **dates**
The **cashews**
The **orange juice**
Juice from one-half **lemon**
A quarter-size piece of the **orange peel**, diced
One tablespoon **vanilla**, or the scrapping from inside one-half **vanilla** bean

Optional:
Pinch of **cinnamon or nutmeg**
If you want the icing to take on a berry color, blend in some **blueberries** or **blackberries**, or a **strawberry** or two

• APPLE COBBLER

In a bowl mix together:
Two or three cored **apples** diced small
Lemon juice from one-fourth of a lemon

Then add the rest of the ingredients:
One-half cup or more **raw oatmeal**
One tablespoon **lucuma fruit powder**
Tablespoon raw **tahini**
One tablespoon **vanilla**
Pinch of pink or sea **salt** (optional)
Big pinch of **nutmeg**
Big pinch of **cinnamon**
One teaspoon **coconut oil** (optional) (melt by putting in little bowl placing that in a pan of hot water)
A little **maple syrup or coconut nectar syrup**

Optional (one or more of the following):
Use **water** instead of coconut oil.
Two tablespoons **buckwheat** that has been soaked and then dehydrated. This adds crunch.
Blueberries. Cherries. Raisins. Currants. Peaches. Bananas. Sunflower seeds. Walnuts.

Good as a breakfast salad. Or, put in pie crust, or in four desert cups.

• PIE CRUST

Process in a Cuisinart
About one-half cup of raw **coconut meat**

Then add the rest of the ingredients to the Cuisinart:
Four **dates**
Three tablespoons **sunflower seeds**
One-half cup raw, uncooked **oats**
One-half teaspoon **cinnamon**
One-fourth teaspoon **nutmeg**
One-half teaspoon pink or sea **salt** (optional)
One tablespoon **vanilla**
One teaspoon raw **tahini** and ...
Three tablespoons **sesame seeds**
Six raw **walnuts**
Eight raw **macadamia nuts**
Two tablespoons raw **carob powder**
Water (very little - minimal - just enough to make the crust stick)

After processing in the Cuisinart, press into glass pie pan and chill.

Fill with your favorite chocolate/carob pudding/mousse, or use as a crust for cheesecake, or raw fruit pie filling.

• FRUIT PIE CRUST

In a Cuisinart, combine:
One-half cup of your choice, raw **macadamia nuts or pecans**

One-half cup raw **walnuts**

Five large dates, or seven or eight small **dates**, pitted

One-half teaspoon **cinnamon**

Optional:
Pinch of **nutmeg and/or** pinch or **cloves**

Combine until all ingredients are well mixed.
Press into a glass pie pan and chill.

Fill with your choice of thin slices of fruit, such as bananas, peaches, pears, apples, and berries.

You can also make a **berry sauce** to drizzle all over the top by blending:
Half a cup of **berries** (either blueberries, strawberries, raspberries,, blackberries)
Flesh of one half of a ripe **mango**
A squeeze of one half of an **orange**

Optional for berry sauce:
One **plum**, pinch of **cinnamon**, tablespoon **Yacon root syrup**, or tablespoon **maple syrup**

• FRUIT PIE FILLING

Core (apples or pears) or pit (peaches) and then thinly slice:
Three **apples or** ripe **peaches or** ripe **pears**

Stir together in a big bowl:
The sliced fruit

An even teaspoon of **cinnamon** (some people like a little more cinnamon)
A small pinch of **cloves**
A pinch of **nutmeg**
Lemon juice from one-fourth of a lemon
Orange juice from one-fourth of a lemon
One tablespoon mesquite **powder**

Optional:
Tablespoon of **maple syrup**
Sprinkling of **sesame seeds**
Top with thin slices of **banana** or **strawberries**

Pour into raw pie crust (from above recipe). Chill.

• FIG BERRY DESSERT

From Julie Tolentino

Take a handful of organic dried **figs** (three or four per serving). Dried figs can be found all year round. Stay away from sulfite dried figs.

Cut off the stems, leaving a small hole around the top. Take one or two halved **pecans** and insert into the hole. Push pecan gently as far as you can inside the fig.

Puree any berry (six berries), preferably **strawberries or raspberries** with juice from one-half of a squeezed **orange**. Puree in mini food processor or blender.

Spoon and swirl berry puree onto light colored dessert plate. Place fig newtons on the swirl of berry, top with **coconut shreds** or **cinnamon**.

213

• STRAWBERRY-BANANA DESSERT

Serves four.

In bowl, stir well with a spoon:
Four tablespoons raw **tahini**
Four tablespoons raw **honey**
One teaspoon **vanilla**
Two tablespoons raw **sunflower seeds**
One-fourth cup raw **buckwheat**

Cut in small pieces:
Two cups **strawberries**

Put the strawberry pieces in the bowl with the tahini, honey, vanilla, sunflower seed, buckwheat mixture. Stir together until strawberries are mostly coated with the other ingredients.

In a small food processor, blend:
The juice from one-half of a **lemon**
Six or seven pitted **dates**
One or two **strawberries**
Two tablespoons **water**

On four dessert serving saucers:
Slice two **bananas** into coins, placing an equal amount of banana slices on each plate. Top the bananas with spoonfuls of the strawberry mix. Drizzle a little of the date sauce over each platter of the strawberry-topped bananas.

Serve fresh or chilled.

• PEACH OR STRAWBERRY TEACUP TARTS

Soak for about two hours in water:
One cup raw **almonds**
Then drain the water.

Crust: In food processor, combine:
The one cup of soaked **almonds** (drained)
One cup **dates**, pitted
One teaspoon **vanilla** (optional)
One tablespoon **hemp seed powder**

Filling: In high-speed blender, combine until smooth:
Several fresh **strawberries or** four ripe **peaches**
Four **dates**, pitted
One-fourth cup **pignolis** (pine nuts)
One-forth cup fresh **coconut meat**
Juice from one-forth **lemon**

Garnish (optional):
Fresh berries of your choice, such as **blueberries or raspberries**.
A light dusting of **cinnamon**.

Divide the crust into eight and press into bottom of teacups (or, if you want to make a full-sized pie, use a glass pie dish).

Add layer of thin slices of either peaches or strawberries. Top with filling.

Chill before serving.

• FRUIT PUDDING

Combine in food processor until smooth:
One **mango**, peeled and pitted
Two peeled **bananas**
One-and-a-half cups of cut **strawberries**
One to three **dates,** pitted (optional)

Optional:
Half teaspoon of **vanilla.**

Chill.

Serve by plain, or garnish with **berries**, a **sprig of mint**, or a dash of raw **carob powder.**

• CHIA SEED PUDDING
From Vicki Veranese of Alchemia Luquid Nutrition Restaurant in Byron Bay, Australia.
Alchemialiquicnutrition.com.

High in omega 3 and a great source of soluble fibre.

In bowl, gently mix together, and soak for one to three hours:
One cup of chia seeds (black or white)
One quart of fresh **juice of choice**, we use freshly squeezed organic
pineapple and **apple**
The seeds of two **vanilla pods**

Combine in a blender:
Two **bananas**
One ripe **mango**
Tiny squeeze of **lemon**

Topping
Fresh **passionfruit**
Shredded **coconut**
Goji berries

Take your desired container, if entertaining perhaps a decorative
glass, and begin to layer the chia seed mixture and the topping, when
full. Sprinkle the topping on.

• LEMON PUDDING

In a high-speed blender or food processor, combine:
Two pealed **lemons**
About one-cup pitted **dates**
The meat of one **avocado**

This can be poured into dessert cups and topped with
fresh berries and a sprinkle of **buckwheat**.

• FROZEN VANILLA YOGURT

Freeze overnight:
One **banana**, peeled
Water into ice cubes

Soak in water for several hours, or overnight:
A dozen truly raw **almonds**. Then rinse.

In high-speed blender, combine until milky smooth:
The soaked raw **almonds**
One teaspoon **vanilla**
One teaspoon raw **sesame seeds**
Two cups **water**

Cut open:
One **Thai coconut** (Google: How to open Thai coconut).
Drain the coconut water into a bowl
Scrape out the white coconut meat into a bowl.

In high-speed blender, combine:
One cup of the **almond milk**
Two to four **dates**, pitted
One frozen **banana**
Four **ice cubes**
One to two tablespoons **vanilla** extract
One cup of the **coconut water**
All of the **coconut meat**
One dash of **cinnamon and/or nutmeg**

Optional:
Add tablespoon of **vegan probiotic powder** to the mixture as it is blending.

Pour into serving bowls, and freeze for one to three hours

• RAW ICE CREAM

Freeze for about a day:
Peeled ripe **bananas**.

Place empty serving bowls in freezer.

In a high-speed blender, combine:
Frozen, peeled bananas – as many bananas as people you are serving
One-fourth teaspoon **vanilla** per banana
One-half teaspoon raw **tahini or raw sesame seeds** per banana
Blueberries or strawberries

Optional:
Bananas should provide enough sweetness. But, some people add a little raw **honey or yacon root syrup.** Some people also add nuts into the blender, such as **cashews** or **Brazil** nuts. I don't. Small pinch of pink or sea **salt** per banana

Put into ice-cold bowls. Eat the raw ice cream right away. It melts fast.

• CANTALOUPE MINT SORBET

From Kristina Carillo-Bucaram of RawfullyOrganic.com and FullyRaw.com

Fully ripen:
One or more cantaloupes (if you eat enough, this can be eaten as a full meal). Wait until your cantaloupe properly

ripens. If you wait until it is soft at the stem end, and smells potent, it will be significantly sweeter!

Cut:
The skin off the **cantaloupe**, getting close to the edge to prevent waste.
Cut the cantaloupe into chunks.

Freeze:
The cantaloupe in a bag or sealed container.

Combine in a food processor:
Frozen cantaloupe chunks
A few **sprigs of mint**
Blueberries (optional)

Scoop:
The whipped sorbet into serving bowl(s), and top with mint sprigs.

Enjoy this sweet treat! Best if savored in the sun!

• SIMPLE CAROB TRUFFLES

In Cuisinart, combine:
One cup raw **nuts (almonds or pecans** – or a mix of both)
One cup **raisins or chopped dates** (or a mix of both)
One-third cup **shredded coconut**
Three or four tablespoons raw **carob powder (or truly raw cacao powder** – or a mix of both [I prefer carob])
Three tablespoons raw **hemp seeds**
Teaspoon raw **sesame seeds**

One-half teaspoon **vanilla**
Pinch of **cinnamon**

Process together until all is combined very well. Should start to form into a big ball. If needed, add one half-teaspoon of **water** as it is processing to help it stick together. Stop. Form into cherry-sized balls. You can also roll them in fractured raw **walnuts, macadamia nuts, pecans,** or **buckwheat**. Chill.

Optional:
If you like the taste of citrus with carob, add one half-teaspoon **orange juice** while the truffle mixture, instead of water. To make sweeter: **Coconut sap sugar**. If you want to make them fancy, roll the balls in either **shredded coconut**, or fractured **nuts** (such as **macadamia**), or **goji crumbles** (in coffee grinder, blend a heaping tablespoon of dried goji berries until crumbled). You can also roll them in **carob powder**.

Serve as a dessert on a small plate with a few truffles, a few berries, and a piece of fruit.

• TRAVELING TRUFFLES

This is a recipe that I made up years ago. Various forms of it have been shared around the Internet and even in recipe books. I used to use
agave in it, but I don't anymore. Instead, I use more dates. I also used to use cacao, but now I use carob. I used to use cacao butter, but now don't, and have increased the coconut oil. People use this as traveling food so they don't get tempted by low quality snack

food. Beware that each spoonful-sized truffle is rich in calories.

This can also be used as a piecrust.

Place all of the following in a big bowl. Stir. Then split in two and process in a Cuisinart:
One heaping handful of **shredded coconut**
One heaping handful of raw, uncooked organic **oatmeal**
Fifteen to seventeen pitted **dates**, cut into pieces
Three of four tablespoons raw **coconut oil** (optional)
One-third cup raw **carob** powder
Two or three tablespoons raw **sesame seeds**
One-fourth cup dried **blueberries**
One-fourth cup **goji berries**
One-fourth cup raw **pumpkin seeds**
One-fourth cup raw **walnuts**, fractured (optional)
Ten raw **macadamia nuts** (optional)
One-fourth cup raw **hempseed powder**
One teaspoon **cinnamon**
One-fourth teaspoon **nutmeg**
One-half teaspoon pink or sea **salt** (optional)
Three tablespoons raw **tahini** (optional)
One to three tablespoons **vanilla**
Two tablespoons **maca** powder
Two tablespoons **mesquite** powder
Two tablespoons **green powder**, such as **spirulina or Infinity Greens**

You might have to add a little **water** (very little – such as one teaspoon) as the Cuisinart is combining the ingredients. You don't want the truffles to be wet, just enough to make them stick together when you press them in your hands.

Optional:
One heaping tablespoon **bee pollen** (unless you avoid bee products).
Two tablespoons of **maple syrup** (which means you can eliminate using the water).

Form into balls the size of cherry tomatoes. Chill. You can also freeze these – which may help prevent you from eating them all at one time.

• CAROB SAUCE

In a Cuisinart, combine:
One-half cup raw organic **coconut oil**
One-half cup raw **carob powder** (or raw cacao powder [I prefer carob])
One-fourth cup **maple syrup, or five soaked dates**
One teaspoon raw **tahini**
One tablespoon **lucuma** powder
One tablespoon **mesquite** powder
One dash of **cinnamon**
One tablespoon **vanilla**
One pinch of **salt** (optional)

• CAROB CRUMBLE

From Theresa Webb of Kitchen Buddy in England. Theresa (at) KitchenBuddy.eu.

In food processor, combine until mixture resembles crumbs:
One cup **walnuts**

223

One cup **dates**
One-forth cup **carob powder**
One teaspoon **Lucuma powder**
Serving suggestions:
For breakfast, combine some carob crumble with nut or seed milk (such
as **almond milk**) and fresh **coconut** and chopped **Brazil nuts**.

Use as a crumble topping to a seasonal **fruit pie** or a **pudding**, such as pureed apple or plums.

BREAKFAST

Monomealing

If you are going to monomeal, the morning is a good time to start.

Monomealing is eating only one type of thing for an entire meal. It may be half a watermelon, or a bunch of tangerines. It might be a big bowl of strawberries, or several bananas.

Monomealing is NOT eating a box of donuts!

Monomeals help rest the digestive tract. As I had mentioned earlier, when I monomeal I often feel a lift in my energy.

There have been many times where I have eaten a large amount of strawberries, and then gone for a long run. For some reason it doesn't work so well with grapefruit.

I have friends who will eat a bunch of dates, and then go on a long run or bike ride. The last time I did it before a run, when I was finished running, my stomach didn't seem to appreciate the dates anymore.

Try monomealing sometimes, starting in the morning. You might carry on with it for an entire day, eating only one type of thing, or making each meal of the day consisting of a different food. Breakfast might be a large bowl of berries. Lunch might be as many apples as you feel like eating. Dinner might be cucumber juice or a bunch of tomatoes.

225

You might experiment with monomealing and see which type of fruit or vegetable works for you. You might find a local natural foods store, organic wholesaler, or farmer who will sell you discount cases of fruits or vegetables, which makes monomealing easier.

• SIMPLE BREAKFAST

Choose one or more:
Berries
Diced sweet tree fruit (apples, pears, Asian pears, peaches, mangoes, bananas, etc.)

Add:
A handful off raw, uncooked **organic oats**
A dash of **cinnamon**
A bit of **vanilla**
One-quarter cup of **water or fresh coconut water**

This is often what we will have for breakfast.

• 48 HOUR BREAKFAST

My friend, Ninaya Laub, taught me this. See: healingjourneys.info

Soak:
One cup **buckwheat** for one to five hours in water. Strain water. Keep buckwheat in bowl, covered with plate.
Rinse twice a day for two days until it germinates (when small root appears).

Combine:
Germinated **buckwheat** (rinsed one last time)
One **banana**, cut into coins
One **apple**, cut into small cubes
Two or three **dates**, cut into small bits

Stir and eat. Germinated buckwheat is rich in amino acids and essential fatty acids. The apple, banana, and dates are brain food.

Optional:
Dash of **cinnamon**. A dabble of **raw honey**. **Raisins**

DRINKS, MYLKS, SMOOTHIES, AND JUICES

• SIMPLE NUT MYLK

Some people spell it *mylk* when they are referring to non-dairy drink.

Some people like to soak the seeds or nuts for several hours in water first.

In a high-speed blender, combine:
Six pitted **dates**
One cup of your choice: **hemp seeds or almonds** (or some of both)
One teaspoon **vanilla** (or seeds from one vanilla bean)
Pinch of **dulse seaweed powder**
Enough **water** to make the milk the consistency you desire.

Chill.

Optional:
Instead of hemp seeds or almonds, you can use raw **hazelnuts**.
Instead of water, use the **water from a coconut** or two.
Add a **banana** or **berries**.

• HOLIDAY NOG

Rinse in water, than soak in water for half a day:
Four cups **Brazil nuts**
Then rinse a second time.

Soak in water for half a day:
Twenty-five to thirty pitted **dates**
Four **vanilla beans**, slit open and cut into small pieces

Combine in high-speed blender:
The soaked **Brazil nuts**
The soaked **dates** and **vanilla beans**
One-half of a ripe **banana**
One teaspoon **nutmeg**
One teaspoon ground **cinnamon**
Enough **water** to make it into a creamy liquid
consistency – about eight cups of water – and more if
you want it to be thinner.

After blending, you can either strain it by placing a
nutmilk bag or cheesecloth into a large bowl and pouring
the contents of the blender container into the bag or
cloth and straining out the pulp, or you can serve it
unstrained.

Chill.

This can be made a day ahead of time to allow the
nutmeg, cinnamon, and vanilla flavoring take hold.

Optional:
One tablespoon raw **tahini**

229

• BRAZIL HEMP MYLK

Soak for several hours, then drain:
12 raw **Brazil nuts** - about 12, raw, NOT toasted or roasted - soaked for several hours, and rinsed.

In high-speed blender, combine:
12 soaked **Brazil nuts**
One ripe **banana**
Pinch of **cinnamon**
Two tablespoons **vanilla**
One teaspoon raw **tahini**
Pinch of pink or sea **salt** (optional)
Pinch of **dulse powder**
Four dates
Two tablespoons **hemp seed powder**
Pour in enough **water** to fill container halfway

Blend on high. Chill.

Optional:
Two or three tablespoons **raw carob powder**
One-half teaspoon **nutmeg or cinnamon**
Berries

• BANANA NUT SMOOTHIE
From Julie Tolentino, a private chef in California.
Julestolen (at) yahoo.com

For this recipe, you can use the nut milk from the previous recipe.

In a high-speed blender, combine until creamy and smooth:

Two cups of **almond milk** (or any variety of nut milk, hazelnut, cashew, hemp milk works as well)

Two frozen **bananas**

One-half cup of fresh or frozen **mango**

Two or three large **kale** leaves

Two tablespoons raw **hemp** powder

One tablespoon **almond butter or tahini**

One teaspoon **agave, or maple syrup, or raw honey, or half a date**

One-half teaspoon **vanilla**

If you want it to have crunchies, after you are done blending, add one of the following, and blend for a few seconds:

One-fourth cup **cacao nibs**

Or, one-half cup fractured **walnuts**

Pour into tall glasses or wine glasses and garnish with a scattering of:

cacao nibs or powder, **hemp seeds, coconut shreds,** and a sprinkle of **cinnamon.**

A delicious treat or meal. I make this smoothie very thick and creamy. Feel free to add more or less of any ingredient to suit your palate.

Serves 2-4, depending on serving size

• BASIC GREEN SMOOTHIE

For more green smoothie recipes, see Victoria Boutenko's book, *The Green Smoothie Revolution*. RawFamily.com. Drink smoothies slowly, don't guzzle.

In a high-speed blender, combine:
Eight leaves **Romaine lettuce**
Eight leaves **spinach**
Two **bananas**
One pinch of **dulse powder**
Enough **water** to make it the consistency you desire.

Optional:
Use **chard** or **kale** instead of lettuce or spinach. **Mango** instead of banana. One **apple**, or **berries**. One-teaspoon **spirulina powder** or **green powder**. One or two **dates**. One tablespoon **hemp powder**.

• SPIRULINA SMOOTHIE

In a high-speed blender, combine:
Two frozen **bananas**
Several frozen **strawberries** (include the leaves)
Coconut water from one coconut
Coconut meat from one coconut
One tablespoon **vanilla**
One tablespoon **tahini**
Three tablespoons raw **carob powder**
Three tablespoons **mesquite powder**
One tablespoon **spirulina powder**

• BLUE GREEN SMOOTHIE

In a high-speed blender, combine:
Two cups **water**
Four **pitted dates**

One **banana**
Several leaves of **kale**
Tablespoon **hemp powder**
Tablespoon freshly ground **flax seeds or chia seeds**
One-forth cup **blueberries**
Half-teaspoon **dulse powder** (or exclude)
One pinch **cinnamon**

• LIVER CLEANSE SMOOTHIE

From Victoria Boutenko, author of *The Green Smoothie Revolution.*
Access: RawFamily.com

In a high-speed blender, combine:
Four cups fresh **dandelion greens**
One-half head **endive**
Two cups **cilantro**
Two cups **apple juice**
One **banana**
Two **pears**
One-inch fresh **ginger root**
One cup **cranberries**

Yields 2 quarts.

• STRAWBERRY-PEACH SMOOTHIE

From Cherie Soria, author of *The Raw Food Revolution Diet*
Access: RawFoodChef.com

In high-speed blender, combine:
Two cups coarsely chopped ripe **peaches or nectarines**
Two cups fresh or frozen **strawberries**

Two peeled **oranges** coarsely chopped
One cup coarsely chopped **kale or romaine lettuce**,
firmly packed
Enough **water** to give it the consistency you desire

Optional:
Two tablespoons **green powder** supplement (such as
Infinity Greens)

• PEACHIE SMOOTHIE

In a high-speed blender, combine:
One or two cups frozen or fresh ripe **peaches**
Half cup or one cup frozen **berries** of your choice
One or two freckled **bananas**
One half cup **water** (or coconut water)
One or two tablespoons **vanilla**
One big pinch **cinnamon**
One teaspoon raw **hemp seed powder**
Two tablespoons **lucuma** or **yacon syrup**, or **two dates**
One teaspoon **green powder** (Infinity Greens)

• ZING SMOOTHIE

Juice:
Six Valencia **oranges**
One **grapefruit**

In a high-speed blender, combine:
The juice of the oranges and grapefruit
Two **bananas**
One cup **blueberries**

A few **strawberries**
One-fourth inch piece of fresh **ginger root**
Tablespoon **chlorella** powder
Heaping teaspoon fractured **hemp seeds**
Heaping teaspoon **chia seeds**

• MANGO ORANGE SPINACH SMOOTHIE

From The Rawfully Organic Co-op, Texas.
RawfullyOrganic.com; KristinaBucaram.com; Kristina
(at) RawFullyOrganic.com; FullyRaw.com.

In a high-speed blender, combine:
One **mango**
Three to four peeled **oranges**
Large handful of **spinach** or **lettuce**
Optional:
For a kick, add either **strawberries** or **pineapple**.

• WARMING SAVORY GREEN SMOOTHIE

From Anand Wells of LiveFoodEducation.com

In a high-speed blender, combine:
Two or three **tomatoes**
One **celery** rib (cut up to make easier to blend)
One-half of a **cucumber**
Several leaves of leafy greens: **kale, spinach, lettuce, or bok choy**
Half a cup of fresh herbs: **parsley, basil, coriander, or dill**

Half of a **lime or lemon**
Palm full of **dulse**
One teaspoon of **kelp** powder
One-forth of an **avocado**
One cup of **water** (or more if you like)
One **chili**
A bit of a **ginger root**, sliced to make it easier to blend
One teaspoon **blue green algae**

Pour into two glasses. Sprinkle with **spirulina**.

• TURQUOISE BARN GREEN SMOOTHIE
From Michelle Premura of upstate New York's
Turquoise Barn retreat. TurquoiseBarn.com.

In a high-speed blender, combine:
One bunch of **Italian parsley**
Two cups **lambsquarters or spinach**
Three cups frozen **mango**
One cup fresh **spring water**
Add more water to adjust desired consistency.
Optional:
One teaspoon **bee pollen**.
Pour in glass and sprinkle with **bee pollen**.

• WINTER GREEN SMOOTHIE
From Victoria Boutenko, author of *The Green Smoothie Revolution*. Access: RawFamily.com

In a high-speed blender, combine:
One cup organic frozen **berries** (any kind)
Two cups fresh **spinach** greens

Two cups **water**
One-fourth-inch fresh **ginger root,** or to taste

Decorate with a **slice of fruit.**

Yields: One quart.

• MELON-MINT COCKTAIL

Soak in water for a few hours:
One-half cup raw **almonds,** then strain out the water.

In a blender, combine until blended well:
The soaked **almonds**
One cup **water**
Several **mint leaves**
Three **beet leaves** (optional)
One cup **watermelon**
One-fourth or small piece of a **banana**
Teaspoon of raw **tahini** or raw sesame seeds
Half teaspoon **vanilla**
Pinch **cinnamon**
Two or three **ice cubes**

• VEGGIE JUICE BASICS

It is always good to make your juice fresh, and to drink it soon after making it.

It is understandable that ideal situations won't exist where you can enjoy the juice right after drinking it. But, if you are to keep it for a number of hours, or days, use a glass or stainless steel jar to keep it in, with a tight cap or lid, and keep it cold.

If you are to bring your juice with you to work or travel, keep it cool.

Put the bottle in a insulated carrying bag, wrap it in a cloth and kept in a cloth bag or backpack, or make a bottle jacket out of a few thick socks.

A friend of mine made bottle insulation sleeves out of cut off old pant legs lined with a couple layers of thick fabric. One end is sewn shut, and the other has a button for closing.

Juices can be frozen (in stainless steel containers, not in glass) so you can take them with you traveling. When you are ready to leave, remove the bottle from the freezer and put in an insulated bag or sleeve. To keep it frozen longer, put that in a backpack or cooler, or wrap the bottle in a towel or blanket and put it in a cloth bag. Depending on the temperatures on the outside, the juice may still be cold the following day.

There are so many types of juicers on the market that it can be confusing to figure which juicer is best for you.

We have an old Champion juicer, and we have a couple of other juicers. The Champion gets used more often. After ten years of use, it was been sent into the company for restoration, and it came back working like new.

We use the left over juicing pulp as a base for making dehydrated crackers. We mix the pulp with flax seeds, and one or more of the following: pumpkin seeds, sunflower seeds, millet, dill, diced spinach, diced red bell pepper, or whatever we can think of that might taste good in the cracker.

Some people have their basic juice that they make with the same ingredients every time. I like to switch up thing and experiment with what might taste good.

If I have a standard juice, it is made out of the following put through the Champion (usually some of the ingredients are straight from our garden):

One **beet**

Several **carrots**

A few **apples**

Several ribs of **celery**

A **cucumber** or two (if in season)

Half a **lemon**

Some fresh **fennel** OR a piece of **ginger** (but usually no fennel and ginger in the same juice).

Sometimes I will then put the juice in the blender and blend in a leafy green, such as spinach, lettuce, Italian parsley, or cilantro.

I might toss in some blackberries, raspberries, or blueberries.

I might also blend in some freshly ground flax or hemp seed powder.

Sometimes I will put in a heaping spoonful of Infinity Greens – if I have them. They are the only product of its kind that I use.

Some people like to juice carrots with oranges or tangerine. That is a nice taste. But citrus go with other vegetables, such as celery or cucumber. Lemon seems to go well with a variety of vegetables.

Some people like coconut water in their vegetable juice. I have a friend who likes to use coconut water blended with carrots. That tastes okay, but coconut water and other vegetables don't taste so desirable – at least, not to me.

Some people like blending tropical fruit in with their vegetable juice. I find that tropical fruit, like mango or papaya, does not create a good flavor when mixed with vegetables.

Play around with your juicer, experimenting with different flavor blends and find the ones that are most to your liking.

Base: Choose one or more:
Cucumber juice
Carrot juice
Apple juice
Grapes

Optional:
Celery
Beets
Fresh fennel

Blend or juice one or more:
Chard
Kale
Spinach
Lettuce

• GREEN DRINK

Juice:
One **cucumber**

In a high-speed blender, combine:
The juice from the cucumber
One **banana**

Two **dates**
Two **kale leaves**
Teaspoon **hemp seed powder**
Several **blueberries**
Teaspoon **dulse flakes**

• GREEN POWER MORNING JUICE

By Chef Cristina Gonzalez of La Vie En Raw Café, Coral
Gables, Florida; lavieenrawcafe.com.

In a high-speed blender, combine:
One cup chopped **apple**
One handful **sunflower sprouts**
Two tablespoons **coconut oil**
One tablespoon **spirulina**
Two teaspoons freshly minced **ginger root**
Four fresh **mint leaves**
Six **figs**
One-half of a chopped **cucumber**
One-half rib of chopped **celery**
One and one-half cups **water**
One pinch Celtic **sea salt** (optional)

• RUNNER'S DRINK

Juice:
Several **oranges**

In a high-speed blender, combine:
The **orange juice**
One chopped **cucumber**

This is a common drink among low-fat raw foodist athletes. You may also like to add one or more of the following:

One **banana**

Several leaves of either **lettuce or spinach**

Berries, such as **blueberries**

A spoonful of freshly ground **hempseed powder** and/or freshly ground **chia seed powder**

A cup or two of **water**

ABOUT THE AUTHOR

Turning to a vegan diet to regain his health after several near-death experiences, and learning the hard way that standard medical care can be anything but health-infusing, John McCabe began writing books exposing the corruption of the medical industry.

McCabe's first book was *Surgery Electives: What to Know Before the Doctor Operates.* First published in 1994, and now out of print, it was an exposé of the financial ties of the medical school, hospital, pharmaceutical, and health insurance industries whose unethical business practices result in the deaths of tens of thousands of people in the U.S. every year. The book was endorsed by some congresspersons and by all of the patients' rights groups in North America.

McCabe also wrote a similar book specific for those considering cosmetic surgery. *Plastic Surgery Hopscotch* was published in 1995 and detailed many of the risks involved with the various surgeries, and in dealing with the medical industry in general.

Realizing that medical care in Western culture is largely the end result of horrible dietary choices centered around toxic processed foods, McCabe turned to writing about how a plant-based diet can prevent and reverse a wide variety of diseases while also protecting the environment.

Becoming an advocate for plant-based nutrition free of disease-inducing animal protein, synthetic chemicals, heat-generated toxins, and rancid and fried oils, McCabe coined the term *raw vegan*, and began using it in his writings on the topic. *Raw vegan* is now an internationally recognized term defining what is becoming an increasingly popular dietary choice of unprocessed, unheated, fresh, organic, plant-based foods free of the components and synthetic chemicals that trigger disease, but rich in the nutrients on which humans thrive in health.

After more than a decade of helping others to write some of the most popular raw vegan books, in 2007 McCabe's *Sunfood Living: Resource Guide to Global Health* was published by Random House and North Atlantic Books.

McCabe is also the author of the reference book *Sunfood Traveler: Global Guide to Raw Food Culture*. It includes a variety of short chapters on various topics and includes a country-by-country list of raw vegan restaurants, cafes, chefs, businesses, and retreats, and also natural foods stores.

Using a wide variety of scientific studies concluding the benefits of a low-fat diet rich in raw fruits and vegetables and free of animal protein, McCabe wrote the 2011 book, *Sunfood Diet Infusion: Transforming Health and Preventing Disease through Raw Veganism*. It was updated in 2013.

McCabe's book, *Vegan Myth Vegan Truth*, was published in 2013. In it, McCabe repurposed some of his previous writings while adding additional chapters and a vast quantity of quotations from a variety of people voicing their concerns for animals and advocating for the health, cultural, and environmental benefits of a vegan diet.

As a way to expose the dire situation of the damaged environment, including from ocean acidification, mountaintop removal, fracking, tar sands mining, clearcutting, nuclear energy, animal agriculture, monocropping, and the spread of industrial pollutants, and to help educate people on the need for a more sustainable society, including the need to shut down the animal farming cartels and stop the GMO companies, McCabe wrote a little book titled *Extinction: The Death of Waterlife on Planet Earth*. In it, McCabe continues his advocacy for a plant-based diet free of synthetic chemicals, and argues for humans to stop mass breeding and killing billions of animals, stop killing billions of wild animals, and to turn to Nature-friendly sources for energy, packaging, building, clothing, and food.

McCabe is the author of *Marijuana & Hemp: History, Uses, Laws, and Controversy*, which details the world's most useful plant and explains how corrupt politicians have worked with corporate leaders to outlaw industrial hemp farming in the U.S. and many other countries. While the book covers many issues relating to marijuana and hemp, it presents information on the need to utilize hemp as a sustainable resource for materials used for construction, and also for making fabric, fuel, cleaning products, biodegradable plastic, and nutritionally rich food.

In this book of easy, simple, no-nonsense recipes, McCabe provides a variety of dishes that are easy to make, low-fat, rich in nutrients, and diverse enough to satisfy a wide variety of preferences.

As an author of numerous books and a ghost co-author of many books by other writers, McCabe has had his hand in more raw vegan books than any other writer. And now, this simple little recipe book that will be a nice addition to the kitchen of any person interested in healthy dietary choices.

With this book, McCabe continues his global influence, playing a role in creating a raw vegan culture that is flourishing in some regions while beginning to blossom in countries the world over.

While California is considered the epicenter of raw vegan cuisine, interest has gone global. From South Africa to Northern Europe, New Zealand and Australia to Asia, and throughout the Americas, raw vegan culture continues to evolve into a force that has become an industry and lifestyle influencing everything from what is being grown on farms and in home gardens, to what is being served in restaurants and sold in stores and at farmers' markets.

To familiarize yourself with the concepts behind raw veganism, read McCabe's book, *Sunfood Diet Infusion*. Combined with his other book, *Igniting Your Life*, implementing its teachings in daily life and awakening the senses through pure, unadulterated, plant-base nutrition can spur a life previously undiscovered, and perhaps one far beyond what the reader had previously considered possible.

McCabe encourages people to plant and protect trees and forests; to protect animals and wildlife habitat; to protect the environment; to practice yoga; to walk or to ride a bike instead of driving a car; to use cloth shopping bags instead of "paper or plastic"; to use biodegradable cleaning and otherwise environmentally safe household and body care products; to work against the genetic engineering of food (such as by such companies as Monsanto and Bayer CropScience); to work for GMO labeling laws; to stop the spread of nuclear energy and creation of nuclear weaponry; to work to legalize industrial hemp farming so it can be made into paper, clothing, food, building materials, energy, and other materials while supporting family farmers; to disconnect from the corporate food chain by planting organic food gardens and supporting local organic farmers; and to live close to Nature by following a plant-based diet consisting of organically grown, non-GMO foods free of synthetic food additives, MSG (monosodium glutamate), and corn syrup, agave, and other processed sugars and salt.

IgnitingYourLife.com
SunfoodLiving.com
SunfoodTraveler.com

To write the author:
John McCabe
C/O: Carmania Books
POB 1272
Santa Monica, CA 90406-1272, USA

"*Igniting Your Life* will kindle your innermost desires and rouse the passionate fire that has been smoldering within you… I believe it holds the promise of being a limitless resource of hope and inspiration."

– **Cherie Soria**, author *The Raw Food Diet Revolution*. Founder and director Living Light International, For Bragg, California. RawFoodChef.com

"In this book McCabe encourages readers to recognize their true potential and work towards a better way of living and being, so all may benefit."

– **Sienna Blake**, publisher, Australia's *Vegan Voice* magazine: Veganic.net

"Amazingly solid information. If I had to pick one book to take to a desert island, it would be *Igniting Your Life*. The number-one book I would recommend to someone to start improving their life."

– **Chris Randall**, RealRawResults.com

"An impressive collection of eclectic quotations and thoughtful commentary. Inspiring and motivating… I'm reading your book again and really enjoying it. You've certainly captured the wisdom of the ages here."

— **Victoria Moran**, author *Living a Charmed Life: Your Guide to Finding Magic in Every Moment of Every Day*. VictoriaMoran.com

"This journey of remembering is constant throughout this book, an uplifting and empowering collection of worldly work. Inspiring conversations arise from those in earshot as you read."

— **Sheridan Hammond**, Australia. Founder and director Samudra Yoga Surfing & Food 4 Life. Samudra.com.au.

"John has collected wisdom from hundreds of people from many centuries. He has organized this and added his own wisdom to create a manual for changing your life for the better. This is a practical book with tasks which, if followed, will improve your life. After only a few hours of reading, I was already writing life plans and lists of things I needed to change in my life."

— **Rob Hull**, publisher, London's *Funky Raw* magazine: FunkyRaw.com; RawRob.com

"We defy you to not be inspired by this book! *Igniting Your Life* is overflowing with both practical information and motivational messages that are clearly the result of a lifetime's worth of research and practice. *Igniting Your Life* is a book that really enables one to 'start where they are' and begin to incorporate its ideas for change immediately. Never before has a 21st century writer combined so eloquently a vision with a tangible blueprint for the holistic healing of the human body and spirit."

— **Matt Amsden**, author *RawVolution*, and **Janabai Amsden**, ELR restaurant, Santa Monica, CA. EuphoriaLovesRawvolution.com

"Where we place our attention determines our experience. If we focus on the news and mainstream media we get negativity, death, and destruction. On the other hand, if we focus on uplifting our spirit and mind we create a completely different reality. To this end I highly recommend that you turn off the TV and read John McCabe's *Igniting Your Life*; it is pure gold! If you are looking for inspiration to improve or change your life, this book is an invaluable companion on the journey. John weaves a commentary full of practical hints, tips, and insight with uplifting quotations from some of humanity's greatest souls."

– **Anand Wells**, Australia's RawPower.com.au and LiveFoodEducation.com

"*Igniting Your Life* is a book written by an independent thinker for independent thinkers. Or, chances are, you will certainly be one by the time you have finished reading it. John has a penetrating and comprehensive view of the numerous ways in which we can all safeguard not only our own health but also, by extension, the health of the environment and the other people and life forms we share it with. To put it simply, he knows what really matters. The huge collection of great quotations that fill his latest book are reason enough to read it, but if we choose to actively ignite our lives in the ways that John suggests, our enhanced energy and clarity will enable us to do more good in this world and also to be a lot happier in the process."

– **Angela Starks** and **Michael Stein**, New York. YogaInTheRaw.com

"If I could ONLY pick one self-help book to read ever again it would be John McCabe's *Igniting Your Life*. A powerful book full of quotations about all aspects of life. A great compilation that shouts inspiration from every page. You can simply flick to any page and you get some supercharg'n info. The more I read it, the more I can relate to it. Gold stuff!"

– **Harley Durianrider Johnstone**, Australian Division One biking athlete and co-founder of 30BananasADay.com

"After a few days of reading and being completely inspired, I wanted to say a huge THANK YOU! Every quote, every paragraph, made me think, 'I want to add this to my next blog' as they resonated so profoundly within me. This book is about to become the first book in the cafe! To ignite everyone's life!"

    – Maya Melamed, Sydney, Australia. ChangingMaya.com.au

"I love your book. Your book has also changed my mum's life. She is now searching for her purpose more than ever. Thank you so much."

    – Freelee Love, Australia; 30BananasADay.com

"Your book is really marvelous. Once again, I hit a quote that jumped my DNA to full attention, and I appreciated it so much I wanted to tell you that you have done a very good thing. I hope your book sets the world on fire. In a good way."

    – Sara Honeycutt, artist & proprietor of New Gallery Studio, Taos, New Mexico; NewGalleryStudio.com

"Really amazing book. One that is tough to put down and one that changes the way people create themselves."

    – Glen Colello, Catch a Healthy Habit restaurant, Connecticut, USA; CatchAHealthyHabit.com

"An enjoyable read with a common sense approach. Gets to the point in a basic, matter-of-fact way."

    – Michelle Premura, Turquoise Barn, New York; TurquoiseBarn.com

 "A wonderful book, one you can resource over and over again for eternity."

    – Hugh Cruickshank, Raw-Foods-Diet-Center.com

"John McCabe has written a comprehensive guide to bringing yourself into alignment with your higher being. *Igniting Your Life* is essential reading, for those looking to evolve in all areas of life. I have this book on my nightstand, to inspire me before I sleep and when I awake."

    – Steven Prussack, RawVeganRadio.com

"John McCabe's books are a constant source of inspiration."

    – Kate Quinn, Australia

Living Light
Making Healthy Living Delicious!™

L IVING LIGHT CULINARY INSTITUTE is the world's leading organic, gluten free, gourmet raw vegan culinary school with programs for individuals, chefs, and instructors.

Located on the beautiful Mendocino coast of Northern California, Living Light was founded in 1997 by Cherie Soria, who is known as "The mother of gourmet raw vegan cuisine." Her graduates are a virtual who's who in the world of raw foods.

People from over 60 countries have attended the institute to study raw vegan culinary arts and the science of raw food nutrition, and become certified chefs, nutritional consultants, instructors, and recipe book authors. Many of the raw restaurants and raw catering companies around the world are owned by graduates of Living Light.

Even though Living Light is a California licensed culinary school, and they train professionals, many of the students are people who simply want to learn to make healthy living delicious foods for themselves and their families. Some turn their stay into a self-styled educational vacation. In addition to attending classes at Living Light, they enjoy the natural surroundings of the Northern California coast, charming towns, artist offerings, wineries, yoga studios, massage therapists, hiking trails, ancient forests, and outdoor sporting activities. Many artists, musicians, and sports enthusiasts, including runners and bikers, live in the region known for its rustic beauty, forested mountains, rocky coast, and wildlife, including whales migrating too and from northern waters.

To subscribe to the Living Light newsletter and receive free recipes and culinary videos, access their site, RawFoodChef.com, and enter your name and email address; then click on "Send me your monthly newsletter."

Besides Living Light Culinary Institute, Cherie and her husband, Dan Ladermann, own and operate several other eco-friendly, raw vegan businesses. They also have authored books, including *Raw Food for Dummies*, which was published in 2013.

The Living Light Café, with its full menu, and the store Living Light Marketplace share the same building as the Living Light Culinary Institute in a restored landmark building in the seaside town, Fort Bragg. The Living Light Inn, which houses students in comfort, is located nearby in a restored historic mansion.

The Living Light Marketplace has an online store providing gifts for chefs and products for healthful living. (Access: RawFoodChef.com/store/marketplace.)

Cherie and Dan have received numerous awards and accolades for Living Light International, including Best of Raw Chef Training Program, Best Eco Friendly Business, and Innovations in Culinary Arts. Living Light is recognized as one of the leading raw food businesses in the world.

Many of the world's top raw vegan chefs have attended the institute, including Chef Ito of Au Lac restaurant in Orange County, California, and Chad Sarno, who has opened restaurants in England and Europe, and many other recipe book authors, food instructors, and nutritional consultants. Many raw food restaurants employ graduates of Soria's institute. (For more information about Living Light culinary nutrition courses access: RawFoodChef.com)

When seeking raw chef training, consider your goals: Are you interested for professional reasons, or simply for fun and to increase your variety of foods and food prep skills? Then consider your options.

If you are interested in creating a new career in the fast growing arena of healthy living and want to own or run a restaurant, café, food truck, or catering service offering healthy food options like vegan and raw vegan foods, or if you have desires to become a private chef – you may want to research the training programs that you are considering, and determine if they are worth the money; how much they charge per hour of training; if the training is hands-on, or if you are simply going to observe "teachers" preparing foods while they talk; and if they are legitimate schools. Find out if they are certified with the state or other government branch that qualifies teaching facilities.

For your professional degree to be of value, you need the best training you can get from a program that is legitimate and maintains consumer protection laws regulating educational providers.

Even if you are not interested in becoming certified as a professional chef, the quality of your education is important – especially if your focus is on health as well as good taste. Living Light Culinary Institute is a fully licensed teaching facility. Access: RawFoodChef.com

•••

In addition to Living Light as an epicenter of raw food, there is also **Samudra**. Located in Dunsborough, Western Australia, the facility runs yoga and surf retreats. Their raw food café and organic store opened in 2008. Chef training courses began in 2010. They have also been adding culinary gardens and fruit orchards to provide the healthiest food possible to their guests and students.

Access: Samudra.com.au.

John McCabe